D1806937

Gourmet Recipes For Slimmers

from

RAGDALE HALL

How to slim with style

COLLINS

First published in 1983
by William Collins Sons & Co Ltd
London · Glasgow · Sydney · Auckland
Johannesburg

Reprinted 1984

Copyright © SM Leisure Ltd, 1983

Recipes devised by Trevor Potter
Dietitian: Angela Steele, BSc, SRD
Illustrations: Chen Ling
Cover illustration: Linda Smith
Editor: Sybil Greatbatch

All rights reserved. No part of this publication may
be reproduced, stored in a retrieval system, or transmitted,
in any form or by any means, electronic, mechanical,
photocopying, recording or otherwise, without the prior
written permission of the publishers.

ISBN 0 00 411271 7

Typeset by Chambers Wallace of Drury Lane Ltd;
printed and bound in Hong Kong by South China Printing Co.

Contents

Introduction

If you love your food but hate to feel your waist-band start to pinch, you will find a lot in this book to interest you. To start with there are the 1,000 calorie menus designed for all those who would like to lose weight without giving up good food. Follow menus 1 to 14 for two weeks or pick out your favourite menus and repeat them; either way you are bound to reduce surplus flab.

To those who have had the pleasure of a stay at Ragdale Hall, the delicious low-calorie recipes in this book will come as no surprise. Ragdale is perhaps the most luxurious health hydro in the United Kingdom, combining as it does the comfort and amenities of a luxury hotel with the most comprehensive range of beauty and health treatments to be found anywhere. It is also a health hydro where the belief is that a slimmer does not have to suffer in order to lose weight; and that, indeed, a slimming diet, far from being penitential, can actually be thoroughly enjoyable.

Would-be slimmers are invariably amazed. They often expect a starvation diet of lemon juice and water, with dragons searching luggage for hidden biscuits and chocolate bars. Instead, they are offered an interesting and varied low-calorie cuisine which is so plentiful and so delightful they are frequently unaware that it is restricted to between 750 and 1,000 calories a day.

The Ragdale food has been described as 'delicious as any you would find in a top class hotel' – a fitting description for the rare beef, lean lamb, trout fresh from the stream and imaginative salads and desserts which appear on the Ragdale Hall menus.

Recipes for the meals served at Ragdale are given in the chapters which follow the 14 dieting menus. Even if you do not need to lose weight, substituting some of these dishes for more fattening meals in your normal menu will ensure you do not gain weight, either. Because the meals are low in fat and sugar and contain a healthy amount of dietary fibre, they are a very nutritionally sound way of eating.

Dip into the recipe sections and you will find meals for one, meals to be cooked in four portions for serving as family meals or for freezing to be eaten later, tempting salads and interesting ideas for cooking vegetables. There is also a chapter of high style, low-calorie recipes fit to grace any keen hostess's dining table. All the recipes have been devised and tested by Ragdale Hall's brilliant young chef, Trevor Potter.

The inspiration behind Ragdale's innovative approach to slimming fare originated with Managing Director, Richard Quinlan. He is himself a highly trained chef. When he arrived to take control of Ragdale some years ago, Richard Quinlan was determined to make a change from traditional salads-with-everything menus to foods that tasted and looked exciting, while remaining low in calories.

Manager Martin Wootton also trained as a chef and together they appointed Trevor Potter – a young chef trained in France and Italy – with a clear brief: to create an exciting, low-calorie cuisine which matched the Hall's reputation for luxury. Guests also benefit from detailed advice on their individual dietary requirements from the resident dietitian, Angela Steele.

A book of the recipes which have given such pleasure at the table and such encouraging results has long been in demand. Here it is, and it carries with it, we hope, the Ragdale message: that low-calorie food can be imaginative, interesting and fun. Bon appetit!

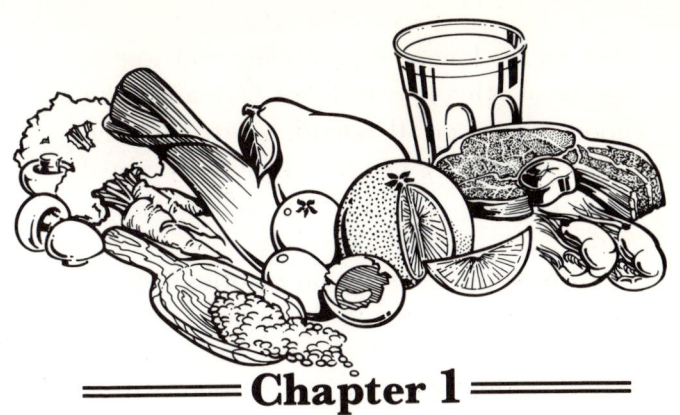

Chapter 1

THE HEALTHY WAY TO DIET

*by Angela Steele, BSc, SRD,
Dietitian, Ragdale Hall*

Many guests come to Ragdale Hall to lose weight and our aim is to show them how this is possible without starving or fasting, but by eating delicious, nourishing food, and the recipes in this book reflect just that philosophy. It is not true that fasting or sipping lemon juice will in any way flush out impurities in your body. Anyone following such an unnecessarily strict regime is not learning how to diet healthily and successfully in a normal environment and is likely to put back any weight lost very quickly. We try to re-educate people into the joys and benefits of healthy food so that they change their eating habits for good.

For their first four days at Ragdale Hall, guests are allowed a daily 750 calories. But they are still served a two-course lunch and a three-course evening meal each day. After four days their daily calorie intake is increased so that by the end of a week's stay they are eating 1,000 calories. This is the lowest number of calories anyone should diet on for longer than a couple of weeks, for below this it is difficult to maintain a good supply of all essential nutrients and vitamins. Many people will lose weight if they keep to 1,250 or even 1,500 calories a day.

Although reducing your calories is essential when you want to shed excess weight, we should not judge every food by its calorie value alone. It is often poor eating habits, rather than the amount of food consumed, which leads to weight problems. With the increase in consumption of convenience foods, often high in calories but low in nutritional value, we are tending to eat fewer natural and fresh foods rich in vitamins and minerals and protein. Also it must be stressed that an overfed body is not necessarily a well-nourished one and too often we eat what we find most tasty without considering if we are eating in a healthy way.

Most nutritionists nowadays universally recommend that the western diet should contain less fat and sugar and more fresh fruit, vegetables and wholegrain cereals, to provide us with necessary vitamins, minerals and dietary fibre. A century ago the consumption of potatoes and flour was much higher in the west than it is now, while the consumption of sugar was much lower. But the tables have turned and we now eat far too much sugar. Artificial sweeteners, on the other hand, are much sweeter than sugar for far fewer calories and do not contribute to dental decay.

The actual proportion of fat in the western diet has also steadily increased over the years and some research has shown that there is a correlation between a diet high in saturated fats (fat from animal source) and heart disease. We need only a very small amount of fat in our diet and it therefore makes sense to cut down on the amount of fat we consume, especially since fats are very high in calories. High fat foods are butter, pastries, biscuits, cakes, chocolate, cream cheese, fatty meats and, of course, all fried foods.

At one time carbohydrate foods, such as potatoes, rice, pasta and bread, were considered to be the most fattening foods, but as long as you don't smother these foods in butter, oil and rich sauces they are now thought to make an important contribution to a healthy diet and modern nutritionists recommend that you get some of your protein requirement from fibrous carbohydrate food, such as beans and pulses.

So you can see how food selection is important when you are dieting. The basis of a healthy eating plan (whether you are dieting or not) is one that is low in fat, sugar, alcohol and salt but high in fresh fruits and vegetables, wholegrain cereals, eggs, fish, poultry, milk, pulses and bread. Fibre too is important in your diet as this not only helps to prevent constipation (something that dieters often complain of) but these foods are also very bulky and filling. Bran, wholegrain cereals, wholemeal bread, pulses, fruit and vegetables are high in fibre.

To slim successfully and keep the weight off, a change of eating habits is necessary. But it must be a realistic change that will fit into your way of life. Eating habits are often established from childhood and are based on many factors other than just satisfying hunger. We eat because we are bored, depressed, or lonely, because it is fun, or we feel we deserve a treat. A diet which therefore rigorously excludes every food that you enjoy is doomed to failure. That is why at Ragdale, and in this book of recipes, we have made the dishes as delicious and tempting as possible.

Think in terms of your diet being the start of a new eating plan that is going to keep you slim and fitter for ever. Crash dieting and following gimmicky diets is not the answer, because, although you may initially start out by losing weight quickly you will not be able to maintain the diet long-term. When you first begin to diet you will have to be a bit strict to get those excess pounds off, but when you have reached your goal by using the menus and recipes in this book, you will have probably developed some good eating habits that you will want to continue.

A realistic weekly weight loss at home is 2lb / 1kg, but some weeks you may lose more weight than others. It is probably best to think in terms of losing half a stone (3kg) a month. Do not weigh yourself every day: the normal person's body water fluctuates daily and so you will not see a true weight loss. Becoming obsessed with the scales only leads to depression if they do not register what you would like. Weigh yourself once a week at the same time of day, wearing similar clothes. In fact, your clothes tend to be a better guide than any scales and losing an inch around the waist can be more psychologically boosting than any scales.

If you wish to lose weight faster, then your best plan is to increase the amount of exercise you take, rather than reduce your calories any further. Exercise not only makes you more healthy and raises your metabolism slightly, burning up extra calories, but is also mentally stimulating and is a good way to lift a depressed mood. We are a lot more sedentary than our parents were and this could well be a contributing factor to the increasing number of overweight people. The less active you are the fewer calories your body requires.

The benefits of exercise are progressive. Gradually build up the time you spend exercising and you will find it becomes easier as you begin to feel much fitter and have more energy generally. It is important to choose an exercise or activity you enjoy so that you are happy to carry it out on a regular basis. It is not necessary to choose something very strenuous, such as squash or mountain climbing (unless these are the sports you really enjoy). Just running upstairs instead of walking up them is a marvellous way of burning off unwanted calories, while going to a regular keep fit class will help to get you into the exercise habit. However, if you suffer from high blood pressure, or are very overweight, you should not attempt the very strenuous exercise of running up stairs – instead, a brisk walk every day will work wonders.

Regular exercise is highly recommended by doctors concerned with the high incidence of heart disease in this country and swimming and yoga have been found useful in treating patients with arthritis. If you think in terms of your slimming plan as being a healthy way of eating (as it certainly will be if you follow the menus in this book) rather than a short-term diet, and combine it with increased activity or regular exercise, then you will be following a programme that will not only help you to lose weight but will make you fitter, healthier and more confident, too.

Chapter 2

RAGDALE DIETING MENUS

The following menus are based on the Ragdale Hall dieting programme. A light breakfast is followed by a two-course lunch and a three-course evening meal, but the order in which you eat these meals is not important. You may, if you prefer, have your main meal in the middle of the day. If you do not wish to eat breakfast, you can save that meal for a suppertime snack. We give a calorie count for each meal so it is possible to make up your own menus using your favourite dishes.

Each of these menus comes to around 1,000 calories and most slimmers will find that they can add 250 calories' worth of snacks a day to this and still lose weight. The only people who may have to keep to a very strict 1,000 calories are those who have been dieting for a long period; who have less than a stone to lose or who are very inactive.

All the menus have been nutritionally assessed and contain all the nutrients and vitamins you need for a healthy diet.

The meals in these menus are delicious enough to serve to family and friends, so there is no need to cook one meal for them and another for yourself. If they have particularly hearty appetites, you can serve them with larger portions, or extra vegetables.

Each day you are allowed 275ml / $\frac{1}{2}$ pint skimmed milk for use in tea or coffee. You are not allowed sugar, but if you wish you can use an artificial sweetener. Black coffee and tea contain a negligible number of calories and can be drunk freely. You can also drink as much water or low-calorie mixers and squashes as you wish.

The recipes for these menus are divided into three chapters in the book. Those marked * are in Chapter 3, Recipes for One. The recipes marked ** are suitable for freezing and are to be found in Chapter 4. They have been given in four-portion quantities so that you can either serve them for the family or freeze them for later in individual portions. Recipes for vegetables and salads marked † can be found in Chapter 5. We have suggested vegetables to serve with each dish but you may substitute these with any vegetables as long as they add up to the same number of calories. A list of vegetables with their calorie values is given on page 61.

*   *Recipes for one*
**   *Recipes for freezing*
†   *Vegetables and salads*

Menu 1

275ml / ½ pint skimmed milk for use in tea or coffee throughout the day: *100 calories*

Breakfast *195 calories*
½ grapefruit
1 sachet Sweet 'n' Low or saccharin sweetener
142g / 5oz carton St Ivel Natural Yogurt
25g / 1oz 30% Bran Flakes

Lunch *240 calories*
Melon Cocktail *
Stuffed Pepper **
Braised Celery †

Dinner *495 calories*
Chicken Broth **
Escalope Pork Hongroise *
150g / 5oz green beans, boiled
Orange Sorbet **

Menu 2

275ml / ½ pint skimmed milk for use in tea or coffee throughout the day: *100 calories*

Breakfast *190 calories*
125ml / 4fl oz unsweetened orange juice
1 slice wholemeal bread
(25g / 1oz), toasted
15g / ½oz low-fat spread
5ml / 1 teaspoon marmalade

Lunch *295 calories*
Consommé Brunoise *
Ham Cornets and Broccoli *
California Salad †

Dinner *370 calories*
Mushrooms à la Grecque **
Plaice Bonne Femme *
225g / 8oz French beans, fresh or frozen
Rum and Raisin Mousse **

14

Menu 3

275ml / ½ pint skimmed milk for use in tea
or coffee throughout the day: *100 calories*

Breakfast   *225 calories*
125ml / 4fl oz unsweetened grapefruit juice
1 egg, size 3, poached in water
1 slice wholemeal bread
(25g / 1oz), toasted
1 medium apple

Lunch   *335 calories*
Florida Cocktail *
Lamb Salad Niçoise *
Mushroom and Cucumber Salad †

Dinner   *350 calories*
Tomato Soup **
Plaice Breval *
175g / 6oz French beans, fresh or frozen
Pear Snow *

Menu 4

275ml / ½ pint skimmed milk for use in tea
or coffee throughout the day: *100 calories*

Breakfast   *220 calories*
125ml / 4fl oz unsweetened grapefruit juice
40g / 1½oz Bran Buds
125ml / 4fl oz skimmed milk
(extra to allowance)
125g / 4oz pear

Lunch   *240 calories*
Prawn and Grapefruit Salad *
Mixed salad of lettuce, cucumber,
watercress
Strawberry Fool **

Dinner   *410 calories*
Baked Egg Princesse *
Coq au Vin **
125g / 4oz broccoli, fresh or frozen
1 apple, orange or pear

Menu 5

275ml / ½ pint skimmed milk for use in tea or coffee throughout the day: *100 calories*

Breakfast   *255 calories*
125ml / 4fl oz unsweetened orange juice
40g / 1½oz home-made Muesli *
125ml / 4fl oz skimmed milk
(extra to allowance)

Lunch   *210 calories*
Cheesy Peach 'n' Pepper Salad *
Orange and Celery Salad †
1 apple, orange or pear

Dinner   *405 calories*
Mushrooms à la Provençale **
Fillet of Sole Véronique *
Green Beans Fines Herbes †
Melon with Stem Ginger *

Menu 6

275ml / ½ pint skimmed milk for use in tea or coffee throughout the day: *100 calories*

Breakfast   *160 calories*
½ grapefruit
1 sachet Sweet 'n' Low or saccharin sweetener
1 slice wholemeal bread (25g / 1oz)
15g / ½oz low-fat spread
5ml / 1 level teaspoon marmalade

Lunch   *300 calories*
Swiss Salad *
Mixed salad of lettuce, cucumber, watercress
1 apple, orange or pear

Dinner   *340 calories*
Corn on the Cob *
Kidney and Mushroom Roll **
Leeks Fines Herbes †
75g / 3oz peas, boiled
Orange Sorbet **

16

Menu 7

275ml / ½ pint skimmed milk for use in tea or coffee throughout the day: *100 calories*

Breakfast   *195 calories*
125ml / 4fl oz unsweetened orange juice
40g / 1½oz Bran Buds
125ml / 4fl oz skimmed milk
(extra to allowance)

Lunch   *280 calories*
125ml / 4fl oz tomato juice, sprinkled with chopped basil
Smoked Trout Ragdale *
Coleslaw Salad †

Dinner   *490 calories*
Cauliflower and Cottage Cheese Soup **
Oriental Kebabs **
Bean Sprouts Oriental Style †
Lychees and Ginger **

Menu 8

275ml / ½ pint skimmed milk for use in tea or coffee throughout the day: *100 calories*

Breakfast   *215 calories*
125ml / 4fl oz unsweetened orange juice
25g / 1oz 30% Bran Flakes
1 portion home-made Yogurt *

Lunch   *285 calories*
Grapefruit Xérès *
Spanish Omelette *
Mixed salad of lettuce, cucumber, watercress

Dinner   *405 calories*
French Onion Soup **
Sweet and Sour Gammon *
Bean Sprouts Oriental Style †
Peach Melba *

Menu 9

Breakfast *170 calories*
Slice honeydew melon (approx. 175g / 6oz)
1 slice wholemeal bread
(25g / 1oz), toasted
15g / ½oz low-fat spread
5ml / 1 level teaspoon strawberry jam

Lunch *315 calories*
French Onion Soup **
Grapefruit Ragdale *
Coleslaw Salad †
1 medium apple or pear

Dinner *375 calories*
Tomato Gervaise *
Lambs' Kidneys Turbigo **
Risotto Rice †
Pineapple with Kirsch *

Menu 10

275ml / ¼ pint skimmed milk for use in tea
or coffee throughout the day: *100 calories*

Breakfast *170 calories*
½ grapefruit
1 sachet Sweet 'n' Low or
saccharin sweetener
25g / 1oz Special K
125ml / 4fl oz skimmed milk (extra
to allowance)

Lunch *255 calories*
Prawn and Tomato Platter **
Leeks Fines Herbes †
1 apple, orange or pear

Dinner *460 calories*
Slice honeydew melon (approx. 175g / 6oz)
Supreme of Chicken Marsala *
1 tomato, grilled
75g / 3oz sweetcorn, frozen
Pear Belle Hélène *

Menu 11

275ml / ½ pint skimmed milk for use in tea or coffee throughout the day: *100 calories*

Breakfast *160 calories*
1 egg, size 3, poached in water
1 slice wholemeal bread
(25g / 1oz), toasted
5ml / 1 level teaspoon Bovril
(spread on toast)

Lunch *275 calories*
125ml / 4fl oz tomato juice
Cheesy Baked Potato *
125g / 4oz mushrooms, poached in water
with a stock cube
1 tomato, grilled without fat

Dinner *335 calories*
Spicy Mushrooms **
Entrecôte Steak Chasseur **
125g / 4oz French beans, boiled
1 apple, orange or pear

Menu 12

275ml / ½ pint skimmed milk for use in tea or coffee throughout the day: *100 calories*

Breakfast *220 calories*
150g / 5oz home-made Yogurt *
1 slice wholemeal bread
(25g / 1oz), toasted
15g / ½oz low-fat spread
5ml / 1 level teaspoon marmalade

Lunch *340 calories*
Minestrone Soup **
Chicken Curry with Rice **
1 apple, orange or pear

Dinner *290 calories*
Gazpacho Soup **
Veal a l'Italienne *
Courgettes à la Provençale †
Baked Apple and Syrup *

19

Menu 13

275ml / ½ pint skimmed milk for use in tea or coffee throughout the day: *100 calories*

Breakfast *190 calories*
½ grapefruit
1 sachet Sweet 'n' Low or
saccharin sweetener
Scrambled Egg *
1 slice wholemeal bread
(25g / 1oz), toasted

Lunch *255 calories*
Baked Stuffed Trout *
Mixed salad of lettuce, cucumber,
watercress
1 apple, orange or pear

Dinner *465 calories*
Chillied Prawns *
Chicken Supreme **
Carottes Fines Herbes †
Green Beans Fines Herbes †
1 small banana

Menu 14

275ml / ½ pint skimmed milk for use in tea or coffee throughout the day: *100 calories*

Breakfast *175 calories*
2 rashers streaky bacon, well grilled
2 tomatoes, grilled without oil or fat
1 slice wholemeal bread
(25g / 1oz), toasted

Lunch *325 calories*
Spaghetti Bolognese **
1 apple, orange or pear

Dinner *425 calories*
Poached Fillet Sole Princesse *
125g / 4oz spinach, fresh or frozen
Pear Condé **

20

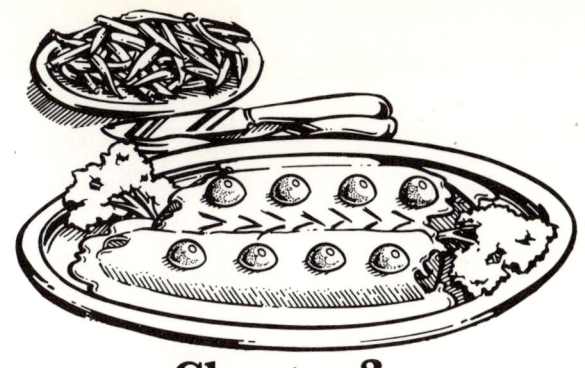

Chapter 3

RECIPES FOR ONE

The following recipes are divided into five sections. First are breakfast recipes, then lunch recipes, followed by three-course dinner recipes which are split into starters, main courses and desserts. Calories per portion are given, so if you are not following the set menus in Chapter 2, any changes can be incorporated into your diet. If you wish to eat with the family, simply multiply these recipes by the number of people you are serving. Choose vegetables to accompany main dishes from Chapter 5, or as recommended in your daily menu.

Throughout this book we sweeten dishes with Sweet 'n' Low which comes in handy sachets each adding just $3\frac{1}{2}$ calories to a recipe. If you cannot obtain this sweetener, any of the other artificial sweeteners may be used, but measure carefully. A little goes a long way and a Sweet 'n' Low sachet is equal to about $\frac{1}{4}$ teaspoon of artificial sweetener. We also use oil-free French dressing and low-calorie salad cream instead of normal salad dressing. Herbs and spices can, of course, be used liberally in your cooking.

Breakfast

Muesli

Makes 25 servings (40g / 1½oz each)
170 calories per serving

350g / 12oz rolled oats
175g / 6oz bran
125g / 4oz chopped hazelnuts
175g / 6oz salted peanuts
125g / 4oz walnuts
125g / 4oz dried mixed fruit
50g / 2oz honey

Put all ingredients into a big bowl and mix well with a wooden spoon. Put muesli into a plastic bag and seal tightly. Shake bag to mix well before taking out a portion. The mixture can be divided into 25 small bags so that it is ready-measured when you want to use it. Keep in a dry place.

MENU *5*

Yogurt

Serves 4   *80 calories per portion*

575ml / 1 pint water
75g / 3oz dry Marvel
30ml / 2 level tablespoons natural yogurt

You will need a wide-necked vacuum flask or a yogurt maker. Sterilize equipment you use by rinsing in boiling water. Boil water and leave 1 pint to cool until it is lukewarm (about 115°F). Whisk in Marvel and yogurt. Pour into flask or yogurt maker. Seal flask and leave undisturbed overnight. If using a yogurt maker follow the manufacturer's instructions. Save 2 tablespoons of yogurt to start your next batch. Revert to commercially produced yogurt occasionally.

MENUS *8* AND *12*

Scrambled Egg

Serves 1   *100 calories*

1 egg, size 3
30ml | 2 tablespoons skimmed milk
Salt and pepper
1.25ml | ¼ teaspoon oil

Lightly beat the egg and skimmed milk. Season. Brush a non-stick pan with the oil. Add the egg and skimmed milk. Cook over a low heat, stirring with a wooden spoon until scrambled.

MENU *13*

Lunch

Ham Cornets and Broccoli

Serves 1   *185 calories*

125g | 4oz broccoli (Calabrese type), fresh
75g | 3oz lean cooked ham, thinly sliced
1 pinch dried tarragon
1 chicken stock cube
275ml | ½ pint boiling water

Trim the broccoli and plunge, stalks downwards, into boiling salted water. Cook for 5 minutes. Tip broccoli into a colander and refresh under cold running water. When the broccoli is cold, fold the ham around it leaving the flower showing. Hold the ham in place with a wooden cocktail stick. Put the ham and broccoli into a casserole dish; sprinkle with tarragon. Make a stock with the stock cube and boiling water and pour it over the ham and broccoli. Cover the dish with a lid or foil. Bake in a pre-heated oven 180°C/350°F, gas mark 4, for 15 minutes. Discard stock before serving.

MENU *2*

Lamb Salad Niçoise

Serves 1   *135 calories*

25g | 1oz cooked lean lamb
1 firm tomato
25g | 1oz cucumber
25g | 1oz onion
2 stuffed olives
½ hard-boiled egg, size 3
30ml | 2 tablespoons white wine vinegar
Pinch garlic salt
Small pinch each dried mixed herbs, dried
tarragon, dried oregano
2 anchovy fillets

Dice the lamb, tomato and cucumber; chop onion. Thinly slice the olives and grate the egg. Mix together with the wine vinegar, garlic salt and herbs. Top with anchovy fillets. Serve chilled.

MENU *3*

Prawn and Grapefruit Salad

Serves 1   *150 calories*

125g | 4oz peeled prawns
5ml | 1 level teaspoon chopped chives, fresh
15ml | 1 tablespoon white wine vinegar
Pinch dried tarragon
½ large grapefruit
½ firm tomato
1 large lettuce leaf
¼ lemon

Sprinkle the prawns with chives, wine vinegar and tarragon, and leave to marinate for 45 minutes. Peel and segment the grapefruit, thinly slice the tomato and shred the lettuce leaf. Put half the grapefruit segments on to a bed of shredded lettuce. Top with the prawns and garnish with remaining grapefruit segments and sliced tomatoes. Serve with the wedge of lemon.

MENU *4*

Cheesy Peach 'n' Pepper Salad

Serves 1   *100 calories*

½ ripe peach
50g | 2oz red pepper
1 spring onion
75g | 3oz cottage cheese with chives

Remove skin from peach after putting it in hot water for a few seconds. Then halve it and remove the stone. Finely dice the pepper and white bulb of onion. Rub the cottage cheese through a sieve, or put through a mincer. Mix cottage cheese with pepper and onion. Spoon the mixture on to the top of the peach and serve slightly chilled.

MENU *5*

Swiss Salad

Serves 1   *230 calories*

50g | 2oz Edam cheese
15g | ½oz cooked ham
25g | 1oz Spanish onion
15g | ½oz dill pickle
25g | 1oz red pepper
15ml | 1 tablespoon tomato ketchup

Grate the cheese; remove and discard any fat from the ham and cut meat into strips. Finely chop the onion and put into a bowl with chopped pickle, chopped pepper and ham. Mix well and stir in the tomato ketchup. Place cheese on a dish and serve with salad mixture.

MENU *6*

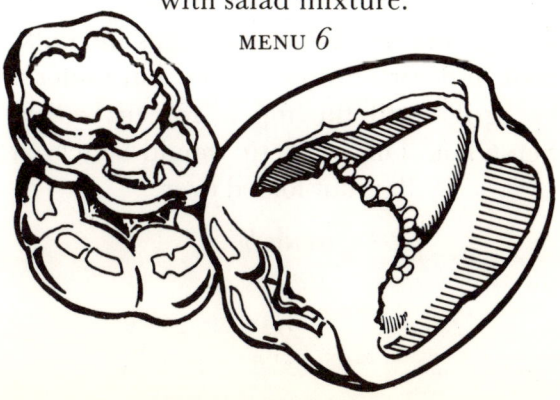

Smoked Trout Ragdale

Serves 1   *160 calories*

1 smoked trout (160g | 5½oz)
15g | ½oz onion
25g | 1oz button mushrooms
Pinch dried oregano or marjoram
¼ lemon

Skin the smoked trout and place it in a shallow dish. Finely dice the onion and thinly slice the mushrooms. Place vegetables on top of the trout, sprinkle with oregano or marjoram and squeeze over juice from the lemon. Seal the dish with foil and bake at 190°C/375°F, gas mark 5, for 25 minutes. Serve hot.

MENU 7

Spanish Omelette

Serves 1   *215 calories*

2 eggs, size 2
25ml | 1fl oz skimmed milk
Salt and pepper
25g | 1oz red or green pepper
25g | 1oz Spanish onion
1.25ml | ¼ teaspoon oil
15ml | 1 level tablespoon peas, cooked

Beat the eggs and milk together and season. Finely dice the pepper and chop onion. Brush a small non-stick frying pan with the oil and add the vegetables. Stir-fry for 2–3 minutes. Pour on the eggs and milk, cook and stir until nearly set. Put under a hot grill until the top is golden brown. Serve hot. This omelette should be served flat, not folded over.

MENU 8

Grapefruit Ragdale

Serves 1   *145 calories*

½ grapefruit
25g | 1oz lean ham
25g | 1oz onion
25g | 1oz green pepper
25g | 1oz boiled rice
25g | 1oz garden peas, boiled
Pinch dried mixed herbs
1.25ml | ¼ teaspoon oil

Scoop out the flesh of the grapefruit, keeping the shell for presentation. Cut the flesh into small pieces. Finely dice the ham, onion and pepper and mix with rice, peas and herbs. Brush a non-stick frying pan with the oil, add rice and vegetables and stir-fry for 3–4 minutes. Mix with the grapefruit cubes, put unto the reserved shell and bake at 190°C/375°F, gas mark 5, for 10 minutes. Serve hot.

MENU *9*

Cheesy Baked Potato

Serves 1   *215 calories*

1 potato (175g | 6oz)
25g | 1oz onion
50g | 2oz cottage cheese
5ml | 1 level teaspoon fresh oregano or a pinch dried oregano
15ml | 1 tablespoon skimmed milk
Salt and pepper

Scrub the potato and bake it at 200°C/400°F, gas mark 6, for ¾–1 hour until soft when pinched. Cut in half and scoop out the flesh, retaining the skin. Finely dice onion and mix with cottage cheese, oregano, milk and potato. Season, pile mixture back into the potato skins. Bake at 200°C/400°F, gas mark 6, for 10 minutes. Serve hot.

MENU *11*

Baked Stuffed Trout

Serves 1   *180 calories*

1 rainbow trout (175g | 6oz)
25g | 1oz onion
25g | 1oz button mushrooms
1.25ml | ¼ teaspoon oil
30ml | 2 tablespoons dry white wine
Pinch dried oregano or marjoram

Ask your fishmonger to gut the trout. If you buy the trout frozen, this will have been done. Finely dice the onion and mushrooms. Brush a non-stick pan with the oil and add vegetables. Cook gently until the onions go translucent. Add the white wine and oregano or marjoram. Simmer gently for 1 minute. Stuff the mixture into the belly flap of the trout. Put the stuffed trout into a baking dish, pour over any liquid left from cooking the onions and seal the dish with foil. Bake at 180°C/350°F, gas mark 4, for 25–35 minutes. Serve hot.

MENU *13*

28

Dinner

STARTER

Melon Cocktail

Serves 1   *105 calories*

¼ honeydew melon (approx. 225g / 8oz slice)
2 small oranges

Cut off and discard skin from melon. Cut flesh into cubes and place in a dish. Peel and segment the oranges and mix with melon. Place in a refrigerator for 15 minutes to allow the flavours to mix.

MENU *1*

Consommé Brunoise

Serves 1   *30 calories*

1 Bovril stock cube
275ml / ½ pint water
15g / ½oz carrot
15g / ½oz onion
15g / ½oz leek
15g / ½oz green pepper
Pinch dried mixed herbs
Salt and pepper

Crumble the Bovril stock into the water and bring to the boil. Finely dice all the vegetables and add to the stock with the mixed herbs. Simmer for 20 minutes. Season to taste and serve hot.

MENU *2*

Florida Cocktail

Serves 1   *110 calories*

1 large orange
1 medium grapefruit
1 sachet Sweet 'n' Low or a few drops liquid saccharin sweetener (optional)

Peel and segment the orange and grape-fruit. Squeeze skins before discarding to extract all juices. Mix segments with juices. Sprinkle with artificial sweetener if needed. Refrigerate cocktail for 15 minutes to allow flavours to blend. Serve chilled.

MENU *3*

Baked Egg Princesse

Serves 1   *100 calories*

4 asparagus spears, canned or frozen
2.5ml | ½ level teaspoon low-fat spread
1 egg, size 3
Salt and pepper

Save the asparagus tips for garnish and chop the remainder very finely. Lightly grease a cocotte or a small ovenproof dish with the low-fat spread. Place asparagus in the dish and top with the egg, taking care not to break the yolk. Season and garnish with the whole asparagus tips. Put the dish on to an oven tray sitting in a little water. Take care not to put in too much water as it should not boil into the egg mixture. Bake at 180°C/ 350°F, gas mark 4, for 10–15 minutes. Serve hot.

MENU *4*

Corn on the Cob

Serves 1   *85 calories*

1 corn cob (approx. 175g | 6oz)
Salt and pepper

Put corn cob into a large saucepan and cover with boiling water. Boil vigorously for 15 minutes. Remove cob from saucepan, drain and serve immediately with salt and a little black pepper.

MENU *6*

Grapefruit Xérès

Serves 1   *40 calories*

½ grapefruit
15ml | 1 tablespoon sweet sherry

Loosen the grapefruit segments, keeping the shell intact. Sprinkle grapefruit with sherry and grill until the edge of grapefruit turns brown. Serve hot.

MENU *8*

Tomato Gervaise

Serves 1   *50 calories*

1 large firm tomato
25g | 1oz onion
25g | 1oz green or red pepper
25g | 1oz cottage cheese with chives
5ml | 1 teaspoon orange juice

Plunge the tomato into boiling water for 10 seconds, then into cold water. Remove the skin. Cut tomato in half and remove the seeds. Finely dice onion and pepper and add to cottage cheese with orange juice. Mix and use to stuff the tomato halves.

MENU *9*

31

Chillied Prawns

Serves 1   *130 calories*

25g | 1oz onion
1 firm tomato
150ml | ¼ pint water
½ chicken stock cube
75g | 3oz peeled prawns
15g | ½oz long-grain rice, raw
Pinch chilli powder

Finely dice the onion and tomato. Make stock from water and stock cube and put into a saucepan with vegetables. Bring to the boil, add the prawns, rice and chilli powder. Simmer for 15 minutes, then leave to cool slightly for 5 minutes before serving.

MENU *13*

──────────── MAIN COURSE ────────────

Escalope Pork Hongroise

Serves 1   *315 calories*

175g | 6oz pork fillet
30ml | 2 tablespoons dry white wine
Pinch dried oregano
5ml | 1 level teaspoon paprika
⅓ stock cube
150ml | ¼ pint water
25g | 1oz onion
25g | 1oz mushrooms
30ml | 2 tablespoons natural yogurt

Trim off and discard the fat and gristle from the pork fillet. Beat the pork until it is as thin as possible. Place on a baking tray, pour on the wine, sprinkle with oregano and paprika. Leave to marinate while preparing the sauce.
Crumble the ⅓ stock cube in the water and bring to the boil. Chop the onion, slice the

mushrooms and add them both to the stock. Simmer uncovered for 10–15 minutes. Take off the heat and add the yogurt, stirring briskly. Return to heat and slowly bring to the boil, stirring continuously. The sauce will thicken slightly (do not worry if it curdles). Remove from the heat.

Place the marinated pork (still on the baking tray) under a pre-heated grill. Cook quickly on both sides. Place pork escalopes on a serving dish. Pour any remaining liquid into the sauce and stir well in. Pour sauce over the pork and serve.

MENU *1*

Plaice Bonne Femme

Serves 1   *240 calories*

2 fillets plaice (75g | 3oz each)
Salt and pepper
25g | 1oz onion
150ml | $\frac{1}{4}$ pint skimmed milk
15ml | 1 tablespoon dry white wine
25g | 1oz button mushrooms
$\frac{1}{2}$ chicken stock cube
2.5ml | $\frac{1}{2}$ level teaspoon cornflour

Put the plaice into a casserole dish, season lightly. Finely dice the onion. Put into saucepan with milk and wine and bring to the boil. Add mushrooms, cover and simmer for 5 minutes. Crumble in the $\frac{1}{2}$ stock cube and stir well. Pour the sauce over the fish and seal tightly with foil or lid. Bake at 180°C/350°F, gas mark 4, for 15 minutes.

Put fish on to a serving dish and keep warm. Pour remaining liquid into a saucepan and bring to boil. Mix the cornflour with a little cold water and add to liquid. Simmer for 5 minutes, stirring and pour sauce over the fish. Serve hot.

MENU *2*

Plaice Breval

Serves 1   *240 calories*

175g | 6oz fillet plaice
25g | 1oz onion
25g | 1oz leek
Pinch dried thyme
Pinch dried oregano
30ml | 2 tablespoons dry white wine
2 firm tomatoes
25g | 1oz button mushrooms
150ml | $\frac{1}{4}$ pint water
$\frac{1}{2}$ chicken stock cube
10ml | 2 level teaspoons cornflour

Remove and discard skin from the plaice. Finely dice the onion and leek and put into the bottom of a casserole dish. Place the fish on top of the vegetables and sprinkle with herbs. Add the white wine, put lid on dish or seal with foil and bake for 15 minutes at 190°C/375°F, gas mark 5. Pour off juices into a saucepan. Chop the tomatoes and button mushrooms and add to the juices with water and $\frac{1}{2}$ stock cube. Bring to the boil and simmer for 5 minutes. Mix cornflour with a little cold water and add to sauce to thicken. Simmer for 2 minutes, stirring. Pour the sauce over the fish and return the dish to the oven for 5 minutes. Serve.

MENU *3*

Fillet of Sole Véronique

Serves 1   *220 calories*

175g | 6oz fillet of sole
150ml | $\frac{1}{4}$ pint water
$\frac{1}{2}$ chicken stock cube
25g | 1oz onion
50g | 2oz grapes
Pinch dried tarragon

Pinch chives
10ml | 2 level teaspoons cornflour
30ml | 2 tablespoons skimmed milk
Salt and pepper

Remove and discard skin from fish and put the fish into a casserole dish. Make up the stock with water and ½ stock cube and pour over the fish. Cover dish tightly with lid or foil and bake at 190°C/375°F, gas mark 5, for 15 minutes. Remove from oven and pour off liquid into a saucepan. Chop the onion, halve grapes and remove seeds. Add to saucepan with the herbs. Bring to the boil and simmer for 10 minutes. Mix the cornflour with milk and use to thicken sauce. Season to taste. Pour the sauce over the fish and put back into the oven for 5 minutes. Serve hot.

MENU *5*

Sweet and Sour Gammon

Serves 1   *210 calories*

125g | 4oz lean gammon
25g | 1oz onion
25g | 1oz button mushrooms
5ml | 1 teaspoon vinegar
Pinch dried mixed herbs
5ml | 1 teaspoon chervil, optional
Few drops Tabasco sauce
Few drops Worcestershire sauce
150ml | ¼ pint water
½ chicken stock cube
5ml | 1 level teaspoon cornflour
1 sachet Sweet 'n' Low

Discard visible fat, then grill the gammon until cooked. Cut into cubes. Dice onion and mushrooms and put into a saucepan with the vinegar, herbs, chervil, Tabasco, Worcestershire sauce, water and ½ stock cube. Bring to boil, cover pan and simmer for 10 minutes. Mix the cornflour with a little cold water and add to sauce with gammon cubes and Sweet 'n' Low. Simmer for a further 3 minutes. Serve hot.

MENU *8*

Supreme of Chicken Marsala

Serves 1   *220 calories*

175g | 6oz chicken breast
25g | 1oz Spanish onion
25g | 1oz red pepper
½ chicken stock cube
150ml | ¼ pint water
15ml | 1 tablespoon Marsala or sherry
10ml | 2 level teaspoons cornflour
30ml | 2 tablespoons skimmed milk

Remove and discard skin from chicken. Thinly slice the onion and pepper. Make stock with water and ½ stock cube and put into a saucepan with the Marsala and vegetables. Simmer gently for 10 minutes. Mix the cornflour with milk and add to sauce to thicken. Simmer for 1–2 minutes. Put the chicken breast into a casserole dish and pour over the sauce. Seal dish with lid or foil and bake at 170°C/325°F, gas mark 3, for 45 minutes. Serve hot.

MENU *10*

Veal a l'Italienne

Serves 1   *155 calories*

125g | 4oz veal fillet
Pinch dried oregano
Pinch dried mixed herbs
Pinch dried basil
¼ lemon
1.25ml | ¼ teaspoon oil
30ml | 2 tablespoons dry white wine

Beat the veal into a thin escalope with a steak hammer. Sprinkle with herbs and squeeze on the juice from the lemon. Put a non-stick frying pan on a low heat, brush with the oil, put in veal escalope and fry gently. When cooked remove from pan and turn up the heat. Spoon the wine into the pan and pour off again almost immediately on to the veal. Serve hot.

MENU *12*

Poached Fillet Sole Princesse

Serves 1   *240 calories*

15ml | 1 level tablespoon chopped onion
30ml | 2 tablespoons dry white wine
30ml | 2 tablespoons skimmed milk
175g | 6oz fillet of lemon sole
50g | 2oz asparagus tips, cooked or canned
½ chicken stock cube

Place finely chopped onion in a small saucepan with wine and skimmed milk. Cover tightly and simmer gently for 10 minutes. Place fish in a small ovenproof dish and pour over onion mixture. Cover with foil and bake at 190°C/375°F, gas mark 5, for 10 minutes. Drain liquid into a blender, add asparagus and ½ stock cube and blend until smooth. Pour over fish and grill for 2 minutes. Serve hot.

MENU *14*

DESSERT

Melon with Stem Ginger

Serves 1   *90 calories*

1 slice melon (approx. 175g | 6oz)
7g | $\frac{1}{4}$oz stem ginger
30ml | 2 tablespoons port

Peel and seed the melon and cut flesh into small cubes. Add the finely diced stem ginger and port. Leave in the fridge for 30 minutes. Serve chilled.

MENU *5*

Peach Melba

Serves 1   *140 calories*

15ml | 1 level tablespoon seedless raspberry jam
30ml | 2 tablespoons dry white wine
1 small scoop vanilla ice cream (25g | 1oz)
$\frac{1}{2}$ canned peach, well-drained

Gently heat the jam and wine in a saucepan over a low heat. Allow to cool. Put the scoop of ice cream into a glass and place the peach half on top. Pour over the raspberry sauce and serve immediately.

MENU *8*

Pineapple with Kirsch

Serves 1   *45 calories*

1 slice fresh pineapple (approx. 75g | 3oz)
1 sachet Sweet 'n' Low
5ml | 1 teaspoon Kirsch

Cut skin from the pineapple slice and cut the flesh into thin slices. Put pineapple in a small ovenproof serving dish, sprinkle with Sweet 'n' Low and Kirsch and bake at 150°C/300°F, gas mark 2, for 15 minutes. Serve hot.

MENU *9*

Baked Apple and Syrup

Serves 1   *70 calories*

1 small cooking apple (approx. 150g | 5oz)
5ml | 1 level teaspoon golden syrup

Core the apple and lightly score the skin around the middle. Put apple in a baking dish containing $\frac{1}{4}$ inch water and pour syrup into cavity. Bake at 170°C/325°F, gas mark 3, for 45 minutes. Serve hot.

MENU *12*

Pear Belle Hélène

Serves 1   *130 calories*

30ml | 2 tablespoons skimmed milk
60ml | 4 tablespoons water
15ml | 1 level tablespoon cocoa powder
1 sachet Sweet 'n' Low
5ml | 1 level teaspoon cornflour
1 canned pear half
1 small scoop vanilla ice cream (25g | 1oz)

Bring the milk and 45ml/3 tablespoons water to the boil and add the cocoa powder and Sweet 'n' Low. Mix cornflour with remaining water and use to thicken sauce. Top the pear with the ice cream and pour over the chocolate sauce. Serve immediately.

MENU *10*

Pear Snow

Serves 1   *60 calories*

1 small pear (approx. 125g | 4oz)
1 egg white
1 sachet Sweet 'n' Low
15ml | 1 tablespoon dry white wine

Peel and core the pear and poach in simmering water and the white wine until tender. When cooked remove from the water and cool. Halve the pear and place one half in a serving dish. Liquidize the other half to a paste-like texture. Whip the egg white with Sweet 'n' Low until stiff. Fold in the pear purée and pour the mixture on top of the pear half. Put under a medium grill until the top goes golden brown. Serve warm or cold.

MENU *3*

=====Chapter 4=====

RECIPES FOR FREEZING

All these recipes are given in four portions.
You may divide them into individual portions and freeze until required; or, if you
are cooking for four people, serve them
immediately.

You may find that certain recipes, the
soups in particular, are well worth cooking
in larger quantities. In this case, double the
recipe and divide into eight portions.

The freezer is one of the best friends a
dieter can have. There are bound to be days
when you have not the time or simply cannot be bothered to cook and it is easy then
to start picking at the nearest, often high-
calorie goodie. If you have a store of
calorie-counted meals in your freezer, it
takes minutes to take one out and pop it
into the oven or saucepan. We give the
calorie counts for single portions, so you
may use these recipes when you choose, to
suit your own diet plan, even if you are not
following the set menus.

41

Lunch

Stuffed Pepper

Serves 4   *145 calories a portion*

25g / 1oz brown rice, raw
4 peppers, red or green (approx. 150g / 5oz each)
227g / 8oz canned tomatoes
125g / 4oz onions
1 clove garlic
2.5ml / ½ level teaspoon dried mixed herbs
125g / 4oz corned beef

Boil the rice in salted water until cooked. Cut the tops off the peppers and discard seeds. Blanch pepper cases for 2 minutes in boiling water, then rinse in cold water. Keep pepper lid. Chop the tomatoes, and put in a saucepan with their juice. Finely chop the onions, crush the garlic and add to the tomatoes with the cooked rice. Sprinkle with herbs and bring to the boil, stirring continuously. Simmer for 5 minutes. Dice the corned beef, add to the tomato mixture and mix together. Remove from the heat, allow to cool slightly and stuff the peppers with the mixture. At this point the lids can be replaced and each pepper left to cool. When cold wrap each pepper in foil and freeze. To serve, take one pepper from the freezer and allow to defrost thoroughly. Put into a casserole dish, still wrapped in foil, and bake at 150°C/ 300°F, gas mark 2, for ½ hour. Serve hot.

MENU *1*

Prawn and Tomato Platter

Serves 4   *165 calories per portion*

227g / 8oz can tomatoes
125g / 4oz Spanish onions
1 clove garlic

2.5ml | ½ level teaspoon basil
450g | 1lb peeled prawns, fresh
Salt and pepper
50g | 2oz Edam cheese
4 small tomatoes

Drain the juice from the tomatoes and save for later. Finely dice the onions and canned tomatoes and simmer in a covered saucepan over a low heat for 5 minutes. Crush the garlic, add to the onions and tomato with the basil and tomato juice. Cover and simmer for 15 minutes. Remove the lid and reduce the liquor by boiling vigorously and stirring continuously. Add the prawns and season. Allow to cool, divide into four portions and freeze. To serve, defrost thoroughly and heat until simmering. Turn into an ovenproof serving dish and mix in grated Edam cheese. Slice fresh tomato and arrange on top. Grill until cooked.

MENU *10*

Chicken Curry with Rice

Serves 4   *250 calories per portion*

250g | 8oz cooked chicken meat
1 packet Knorr Thick Chicken Broth
1 onion
50g | 2oz carrots
1 stick celery
15ml | 1 tablespoon tomato purée
30ml | 2 tablespoons curry powder
1 apple
5ml | 1 teaspoon dried mixed fruit
125g | 4oz brown rice, raw

Discard skin from chicken and cut flesh into small pieces. Make up chicken broth as instructed on packet. Peel and dice onion, carrot and celery and add to soup with tomato purée and curry powder. Simmer for 10 minutes. Add chicken with diced apple and mixed fruit. Simmer for 20 minutes. Divide into four portions and freeze. To serve, take a portion from the freezer and heat in a saucepan. Cook 25g/1oz rice, weighed dry, per person.

Spaghetti Bolognese

Serves 4   *275 calories per portion*

350g / 12oz lean minced beef
227g / 8oz canned tomatoes
125g / 4oz onions
1 clove garlic
5ml / 1 level teaspoon mixed herbs,
fresh or dried
5ml / 1 level teaspoon oregano, fresh or dried
125ml / 4fl oz dry white wine
15ml / 1 level tablespoon tomato purée
125g / 4oz spaghetti, raw

Cook the mince in a non-stick pan without added fat. When cooked, drain off all the fat that cooks out. Strain juice from the canned tomatoes and put into a saucepan. Finely dice the drained tomatoes and onions. Add to the tomato juice and simmer gently while you add the crushed garlic, herbs, minced beef and wine. Cover and simmer for 10 minutes, then stir in the tomato purée. Allow to cool, then divide into four portions and freeze. To serve, heat Bolognese sauce in a small saucepan. Weigh out 25g / 1oz spaghetti per portion and boil in salted water until cooked. Drain and top with hot sauce.

MENU *14*

Dinner

STARTER

Chicken Broth

Serves 4   *70 calories per portion*

125g | 4oz onions
125g | 4oz leeks
75g | 2oz carrots
2 chicken stock cubes
850ml | 1½ pints water
125g | 4oz chicken drumstick, skin removed
5ml | 1 level teaspoon dried mixed herbs
15g | ½oz barley (soaked overnight)

Finely dice the onions, leeks and carrots. Crumble stock cubes into water and bring to the boil. Add the diced vegetables, chicken and herbs. Simmer for 30 minutes then remove the chicken. Add the barley and bring back to the boil. Strip the meat from the chicken and dice finely. Add the meat to the broth and simmer for 20 minutes more.

Allow to cool, then freeze in individual portions. To serve, take a portion from freezer and allow to defrost. Re-heat in a small saucepan.

MENU *1*

Tomato Soup

Serves 4   *35 calories per portion*

50g | 2oz onion
50g | 2oz leek
50g | 2oz carrots
275ml | ½ pint water
2 chicken stock cubes
Pinch dried basil
15ml | 1 level tablespoon tomato purée
275ml | ½ pint tomato juice

45

2 *drops Worcestershire sauce*
Salt and pepper

Finely dice the vegetables and put into a saucepan with water, chicken stock cubes and basil. Bring to the boil and simmer for 10 minutes. Add the tomato purée and tomato juice and simmer for another 10 minutes. Add the Worcestershire sauce and season to taste. Divide into four portions and freeze. To serve, heat from frozen over a low heat, stirring frequently.

MENU *3*

Gazpacho Soup

Serves 4   *40 calories per portion*

227g | 8oz can tomatoes
175g/6oz Spanish onions
½ small cucumber
1 clove garlic
125ml | 4fl oz dry white wine
5ml | 1 level teaspoon mixed herbs, fresh or dried
5ml | 1 level teaspoon oregano, fresh or dried
275ml | ½ pint water
1 chicken stock cube
2 drops Tabasco sauce

Strain the juice from the canned tomatoes into a saucepan. Dice the onions and the cucumber and add to tomato juice with crushed garlic, wine, mixed herbs, oregano, water and chicken stock cube. Bring to the boil, cover and simmer for 20 minutes. Dice tomatoes and add to soup. Allow to cool. Divide into four portions and freeze. To serve, defrost thoroughly, add the Tabasco sauce and serve chilled.

MENU *12*

Cauliflower and Cottage Cheese Soup

Serves 4   *60 calories per portion*

1½ chicken stock cubes
425ml | ¾ pint water
225g | 8oz cauliflower florets
175g | 6oz cottage cheese
Pinch dried oregano or marjoram

Crumble stock cubes into the water and bring to the boil. Add the cauliflower and cook until soft. Remove the cauliflower and liquidize with the cheese until a creamy texture has been attained. Pour the cheese and cauliflower into the stock, add the oregano or marjoram and simmer for 5 minutes. Allow to cool, divide into four portions and freeze. To serve, take a portion from the freezer and re-heat in a small saucepan.

MENU *7*

French Onion Soup

Serves 4   *25 calories per portion*

225g | 8oz Spanish onions
1.25ml | ¼ teaspoon oil
5ml | 1 level teaspoon mixed herbs, fresh or dried
5ml | 1 level teaspoon oregano, fresh or dried
575ml | 1 pint water
2 stock cubes

Thinly slice the onions. Gently fry in a non-stick pan brushed with oil until they begin to brown. Place in a saucepan and add the herbs, water and stock cubes. Bring to the boil and simmer for 20 minutes. Allow to cool, then divide into four portions and freeze. To serve, defrost a portion and heat in a small saucepan.

MENU *8*

Minestrone Soup

Serves 4   *100 calories per portion*

227g | 8oz can tomatoes
125g | 4oz onions
50g | 2oz button mushrooms
25g | 1oz French beans
50g | 2oz carrots
3 beef stock cubes
850ml | 1½ pints water
25g | 1oz peas
5ml | 1 level teaspoon dried mixed herbs
5ml | 1 level teaspoon dried oregano
50g | 2oz spaghetti, raw

Strain the juice from the canned tomatoes into a saucepan. Dice the onions, mushrooms, beans and carrots. Put into the saucepan with stock cubes and water, bring to the boil and simmer for 10 minutes. Chop tomatoes and add to pan with peas, mixed herbs and oregano. Break up the spaghetti, add to the stock and simmer for 20 minutes. Allow to cool. Divide into four portions and freeze. To serve, take a portion from the freezer and heat in a small saucepan.

MENU *12*

48

Mushrooms à la Grecque

Serves 4   *40 calories per portion*

1 clove garlic
125g | 4oz green peppers
125g | 4oz onions
125ml | 4fl oz dry white wine
2.5ml | ½ level teaspoon dried oregano
2.5ml | ½ level teaspoon dried tarragon
275g | 10oz button mushrooms
Salt and pepper
15ml | 1 tablespoon oil-free French dressing
per portion

Crush the garlic; dice the peppers and onions. Put into a saucepan with the wine, oregano and tarragon and bring to the boil. Add the whole mushrooms, cover pan with a lid and simmer for 10 minutes. Season to taste and allow to cool. When cold divide into four portions and freeze. To serve, take a portion from the freezer and leave to defrost. Add 15ml / 1 tablespoon of oil-free French dressing to each portion and serve chilled.

MENU *2*

Spicy Mushrooms

Serves 4   *40 calories per portion*

350g | 12oz button mushrooms
25g | 1oz   low fat spread
½ lemon
5ml | 1 level teaspoon dried mixed herbs
2.5ml | ½ level teaspoon dried oregano or
marjoram
30ml | 2 tablespoons wine vinegar
Salt and pepper

Wash the mushrooms. Melt the low-fat spread in a saucepan. Squeeze in the juice from the lemon. Add mixed herbs, oregano, wine vinegar and mushrooms. Season to taste, cover the pan with a lid and cook gently for 15 minutes. Leave to cool. Divide into four portions and freeze. To serve, allow to defrost and serve cold or re-heat gently in a saucepan and serve hot.

MENU *11*

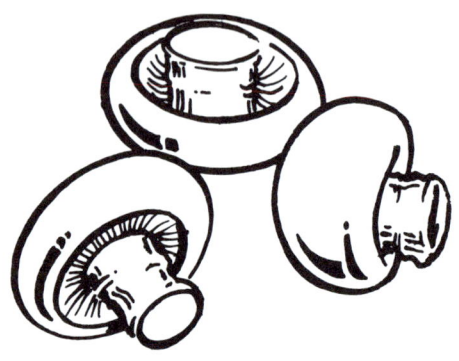

Mushrooms à la Provençale

Serves 4   *45 calories per portion*

227g / 8oz can tomatoes
125g / 4oz onions
1 clove garlic
Pinch dried oregano
125ml / 4fl oz dry white wine
340g / 12oz button mushrooms
Salt and pepper
Wedges of lemon or Tabasco sauce

Sieve tomatoes and discard seeds. Place purée in a saucepan. Chop the onions and add to the purée with crushed garlic and oregano. Bring to the boil. Boil vigorously; add the wine and the mushrooms, cover and simmer for 10 minutes. Season to taste and allow to cool. When cold divide into four portions and freeze. To serve, allow to defrost and serve chilled with a wedge of lemon. Or allow to defrost and heat gently in a saucepan; serve hot spiced with Tabasco sauce to taste.

MENU *5*

Coq au Vin

Serves 4   *230 calories per portion*

4 chicken leg joints (225g | 8oz each)
125ml | 4fl oz red wine
125g | 4oz button mushrooms
125g | 4oz button onions
1 clove garlic
2.5ml | ½ teaspoon dried mixed herbs
1 bay leaf
1 bouquet garni
575ml | 1 pint water
2 chicken stock cubes
227g | 8oz can tomatoes
25g | 1oz cornflour

Remove and discard skin from chicken portions. Put the wine in a pan and bring to the boil. Add the mushrooms and peeled button onions. Crush the garlic, add to the pan with herbs, bay leaf, bouquet garni, 275ml / ½ pint water and 1 chicken stock cube. Bring to the boil and simmer for 10 minutes. Pour the juice from the tomatoes into the stock; dice the tomatoes and add. Bring back to boil and cook briskly, un-covered, to reduce the amount by half. Add the rest of water and remaining stock cube. Bring to boil and simmer for 5 minutes. Put the chicken in a casserole dish, pour on the sauce and bake at 175°C/375°F, gas mark 5, for 1 hour. Strain the sauce into a pan. Mix cornflour with a little cold water and add to sauce to thicken. Pour sauce back over the chicken and return to the oven for 5 minutes. Divide into four portions, cool thoroughly and freeze. To serve, take a portion from the freezer and allow to de-frost. Put in a casserole dish and heat at 190°C/375°F, gas mark 5, for 30 minutes.

Kidney and Mushroom Roll

Serves 4   *95 calories per portion*

225g | 8oz lambs' kidneys
175g | 6oz mushrooms
125g | 4oz Spanish onions
150ml | ¼ pint water
1 beef stock cube
Pinch dried mixed herbs
5ml | 1 level teaspoon dried oregano or marjoram
15ml | 1 tablespoon soy sauce
Salt and pepper
15ml | 1 level tablespoon cornflour
4 large cabbage leaves

Halve and core the kidneys, then thinly slice. Slice mushrooms and dice the onions. Put the water and stock cube in a saucepan and add kidneys, mushrooms and onions, herbs and soy sauce. Bring to boil and simmer for 30 minutes. Season if necessary. Mix cornflour with a little cold water and add to mixture, stirring until it thickens. Leave until cold. Blanch the cabbage leaves by plunging into boiling salted water for 5 minutes. Rinse in running water until cold. Put the leaves flat on a table. In the centre of each put a quarter of the kidney stuffing. Fold over the edges of the cabbage, enveloping the stuffing. Put into an oven-proof dish so the folded side is face down. Pour in enough water to come ¼ inch up the side of the dish. Bake at 180°C/350°F, gas mark 4, for 20 minutes. Cool; wrap in four parcels and freeze. To serve, allow Kidney and Mushroom Roll to defrost and reheat in oven for 10–15 minutes at 180°C/350°F, gas mark 4.

MENU 6

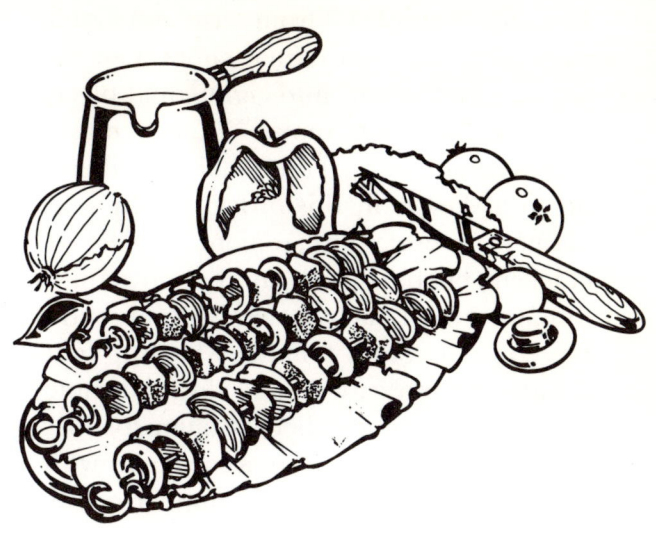

Oriental Kebabs

Serves 4   *265 calories per portion*

Kebabs
125g | 4oz lean pork (preferably fillet)
125g | 4oz lean beef (sirloin or fillet)
125g | 4oz lean lamb (best-end or leg)
175g | 6oz chicken breast
150g | 5oz red peppers
125g | 4oz onions
2 firm tomatoes
8 button mushrooms

Sauce
50g | 2oz onion
½ red or green pepper
50g | 2oz button mushrooms
125ml | 4fl oz dry white wine
575ml | 1 pint water
2 beef stock cubes
Pinch dried tarragon
1 bay leaf
2 drops Tabasco sauce
5ml | 1 level teaspoon tomato purée
2 drops Worcestershire sauce
5ml | 1 teaspoon soy sauce
15ml | 1 level tablespoon cornflour

Discard all visible fat from meat and divide each piece into four equal cubes. Cut the peppers and onions into eight equal pieces and quarter each tomato. Leave mushrooms whole. Thread the kebab ingredients on to a skewer in this order: mushroom; pepper; a beef cube; onion; a piece of chicken; pepper; pork; mushroom; lamb; tomato. Finish each skewer with an extra piece of onion and tomato. Make up four kebabs and freeze, wrapped closely in cling film. To make sauce: dice the onion, pepper and mushrooms. Put into a saucepan with the white wine. Cover and simmer gently for 4–5 minutes. Add the water and stock cube and bring to the boil. Add the tarragon and bay leaf, Tabasco, tomato purée, Worcestershire and soy sauce. Cover and simmer gently for 15 minutes. Mix the cornflour with a little cold water and add to sauce to thicken. Simmer for a further 10 minutes, uncovered, then reduce the volume by a third by boiling vigorously. Divide into four portions, cool and freeze. To serve, defrost kebab thoroughly and sprinkle with salt, pepper and soy sauce. Grill, turning frequently, until cooked. Heat a portion of sauce in a small pan and serve over kebabs.

MENU 7

Lambs' Kidneys Turbigo

Serves 4   *165 calories per portion*

275g | 10oz lambs' kidneys
75g | 3oz pork chipolata sausages
125g | 4oz Spanish onions
125g | 4oz button mushrooms
125ml | 4fl oz red wine
1.25ml | ¼ level teaspoon dried oregano or marjoram

10ml / 2 level teaspoons tomato purée
· 1 beef stock cube
½ pint water
15g / ½oz cornflour

Slice the kidneys, discarding white cores. Well grill the sausages and cut into thick slices. Roughly chop the onions and mushrooms. Put vegetables in a saucepan with red wine, oregano or marjoram and tomato purée. Simmer for 3–4 minutes taking care not to boil off all the liquid. Add the stock cube and water and bring to the boil. Cover and simmer for 10 minutes. Add the kidneys and sausages to the sauce and simmer covered for 30 minutes. Mix cornflour with a little cold water and add to sauce, stirring continuously to thicken. Simmer for 10 more minutes. Cool, divide into four portions and freeze. To serve, allow portion to defrost then heat gently in a saucepan.

MENU *9*

Entrecôte Steak Chasseur

Serves 4   *235 calories per portion*

227g / 8oz can tomatoes
125ml / 4fl oz white wine
2.5ml / ½ teaspoon tarragon
½ beef stock cube
50g / 2oz Spanish onion
50g / 2oz button mushrooms
Salt and pepper
125g / 4oz lean sirloin steak per person
(buy fresh when needed)

Strain the tomato juice into a saucepan, add the white wine, tarragon and stock cube. Cover and simmer for 5 minutes. Dice the onion, mushrooms and tomatoes and add to the sauce. Boil vigorously for 5 minutes, stirring continuously. Season to taste. Cool, divide the sauce into four portions and freeze. To serve, leave sauce to defrost at room temperature then heat in a small pan until simmering. Grill the steak and top with a portion of hot chasseur sauce.

MENU 11

Chicken Supreme

Serves 4   225 calories per portion

4 chicken breasts (approx. 150g | 5oz each)
125g | 4oz button onions
50g | 2oz button mushrooms
125ml | 4fl oz dry white wine
2.5ml | $\frac{1}{2}$ teaspoon mixed herbs
575ml | 1 pint water
2 chicken stock cubes
25g | 1oz cornflour
275ml | $\frac{1}{2}$ pint skimmed milk
Salt and pepper

Remove and discard skin from chicken breasts. Put chicken into a casserole dish and bake at 160°C/325°F, gas mark 3, for 10 minutes. Peel the onions and wash mushrooms. Put into a saucepan with the wine and simmer gently for 5 minutes. Add the herbs, water and stock cubes; simmer for 5 minutes. Mix the cornflour with a little of the milk and add to sauce with remaining milk. Bring to the boil, stirring all the time. Pour the sauce over the chicken, cover with a lid or seal with foil and return to oven for 1 hour. Season. Allow to cool, then divide into four portions and freeze. To serve, allow chicken portion to defrost. Put into a casserole dish and heat at 190°C/375°F, gas mark 5, for 25 minutes or until hot.

MENU 13

DESSERT

Orange Sorbet

Serves 4   *75 calories per portion*

4 oranges
1 lemon
7g | ¼oz gelatine powder
2 egg whites
4 packets Sweet 'n' Low

Grate the skin from the oranges and lemon into a bowl. Squeeze the juice of the fruits over the grated rind and leave overnight. Strain the juice and pour into a bowl and sprinkle on the gelatine. Leave to soak for 5 minutes then stand the bowl in a pan of simmering water until gelatine dissolves. Pour into dish and freeze until mushy. Take from freezer and whisk. Whisk egg whites with the Sweet 'n' Low until stiff. Fold into the juice and return to the freezer. Leave for 15 minutes, then whisk vigorously. Repeat this every 30 minutes until set. The sorbet can then be kept in the freezer until required.

MENU *1*

Lychees and Ginger

Serves 4   *85 calories per portion*

25g | 1oz stem ginger
30ml | 2 tablespoons brandy
275g | 10oz lychees, canned

Finely dice the ginger, cover with brandy and leave to stand for 15 minutes. Put the lychees and juice into a saucepan and boil vigorously to reduce the juice by half, stirring occasionally. Add the brandy and ginger. Divide into four portions, cool and freeze. To serve, defrost at room temperature. Serve cold or gently heated.

MENU *7*

Rum and Raisin Mousse

Serves 4   *75 calories per portion*

25g | 1oz raisins
15g | ½oz gelatine powder
275ml | ½ pint skimmed milk
4 egg whites
6 packets Sweet 'n' Low
3 drops rum essence

Chop the raisins and soak in water over-night. Sprinkle gelatine on to 45ml/3 tablespoons water in a small basin and leave to soak for 5 minutes. Stand in a pan of simmering water until gelatine dissolves. Stir into milk. Whisk the egg whites with the Sweet 'n' Low until stiff. Fold in the milk, rum essence and drained raisins. Put into a plastic container and freeze. After 15 minutes, gently fold together the mixture again. Do this every 15 minutes until the mousse is set. Leave in the freezer until required. Defrost thoroughly before eating.

MENU *2*

Strawberry Fool

Serves 4   *70 calories per portion*

175g | 6oz strawberries, fresh or frozen
7g | ¼oz powdered gelatine
125ml | 4fl oz water
2 small cartons or 300g | 11oz natural yogurt
2 egg whites
4 packets Sweet 'n' Low

If the strawberries are frozen, defrost thoroughly. Dissolve the gelatine in water according to the instructions on the packet and leave until just warm. Liquidize the strawberries to a purée, add the yogurt and blend together. Pour in the gelatine. Blend together and chill for 45 minutes. Whisk the egg whites and Sweet 'n' Low together until stiff. Fold in the strawberry mixture, divide into four portions and freeze. To serve, allow a portion to defrost.

MENU *4*

Pear Condé

Serves 4   *125 calories per portion*

2 whole pears (approx. 142g / 5oz each)
8 sachets Sweet 'n' Low
275ml / ½ pint skimmed milk
50g / 2oz pudding or short-grain rice
30ml / 2 level tablespoons lemon curd

Peel and poach the pears in 275ml / ½ pint water with 4 sachets Sweet 'n' Low until soft (about 10–15 minutes). Drain and reserve the liquid. Allow pears to cool, then halve and core. Mix the reserved liquid with the milk and bring to the boil. Add the pudding rice and 4 sachets Sweet 'n' Low. Cover and cook over a low heat for ¾ hour. Remove lid and cook for 15 minutes longer until thick. Put the rice in a serving dish and top with the pear halves. Heat the lemon curd and spoon over the top of the pears and freeze. Serve immediately.

MENU *14*

Chapter 5

VEGETABLES AND SALADS

Vegetables and salads play an important part in any slimming diet. To open this chapter there is a list of very low-calorie vegetables which can be served lightly boiled in quantities as large as you wish. The recipes that follow show just how inventive you can be when cooking vegetables and still serve up few calories. In the 14 dieting menus (Chapter 2) we specify the vegetables to be served at each meal, but you can choose alternatives from the recipes given here. These recipes all serve four, so that you can share them with your family, but if you are eating alone reduce the amount you cook. We have assumed that two vegetables will be served with most meals, but if you prefer you may have a double portion of just one vegetable.

British salads have a poor reputation, since they often consist of a limp lettuce leaf and a few slices of cucumber and tomato, relying heavily on high-calorie dressings to add interest! The salad recipes here and in Chapter 3 (*Recipes for One*) show that a salad need not be boring. Although the salads in this chapter are intended as accompaniments to a meal some will also make attractive starters to serve before a main course. Quantities are for one but if you are catering for more than one they can be increased accordingly.

All the following vegetables are low in calories and can be eaten in reasonably large quantities. To cook most vegetables, boil a little water, season lightly with salt and pepper and add the vegetables. Bring back to the boil, then simmer until the vegetables are lightly cooked but still crisp. Do *not* overcook vegetables or you will lose a lot of their flavour, natural goodness and vitamins. Mushrooms can be poached in a little stock or lemon juice, or grilled without fat. Tomatoes too should be grilled without fat or, if you wish, you can brush them with $1.25ml/\frac{1}{4}$ teaspoon oil, which costs 10 calories.

Calories per 25g / 1oz, raw weight

Asparagus	5
Aubergines	4
Bean Sprouts	5
Broccoli	7
Brussel Sprouts	7
Cabbage	6
Carrots	6
Cauliflower	4
Courgettes	4
French Beans	2
Runner Beans	7
Leeks	9
Marrow	5
Mushrooms	4
Spinach	9
Spring Greens	3
Tomatoes	4

Vegetables

Braised Celery

Serves 1   *20 calories*

2 sticks celery
275ml | ½ pint water
1 chicken stock cube
5ml | 1 level teaspoon chopped dried chives

Wash the celery thoroughly and cut into small even pieces. Make stock from water and stock cube. Put celery into an ovenproof dish, sprinkle with chives and pour on the stock cube and water. Cover dish and bake at 180°C/350°F, gas mark 4, for 1–1¼ hours. Serve hot.

MENU *1*

Bean Sprouts Oriental Style

Serves 4   *20 calories per portion*

350g | 12oz bean sprouts
50g | 2oz onion
50g | 2oz mushrooms
175ml | 6fl oz water
5ml | 1 teaspoon soy sauce

Wash bean sprouts; dice onion and mushrooms. Bring the water to boil in a saucepan and add soy sauce. Add onion and mushrooms and simmer for 5 minutes. Add bean sprouts and simmer for 5 minutes longer. Drain and serve hot.

MENU *7*

Green Beans Fines Herbes

Serves 4   *25 calories per portion*

5ml | 1 level teaspoon mixed herbs, fresh or dried
5ml | 1 level teaspoon oregano, fresh or dried
Pinch tarragon, fresh or dried
Apple juice (optional)

350g | 12oz runner beans, frozen
1.25ml | ¼ teaspoon oil

Soak dried herbs overnight in a little water or apple juice. Allow beans to defrost or boil quickly for a few minutes and drain. Stir-fry beans for 1 minute in a pan brushed with oil. Add the herbs and continue stir-frying until beans are cooked (about 4–5 minutes). Serve hot.

MENUS *5* AND *13*

Carottes Fines Herbes

Serves 2   *20 calories per portion*

225g | 8oz carrots, fresh
275ml | ½ pint water
1 chicken stock cube
5ml | 1 level teaspoon chopped chives
5ml | 1 level teaspoon oregano, fresh or dried
Salt and pepper

Peel and cut the carrots into thin fingers. Cook in boiling water with chicken stock cube for 5 minutes. Add herbs and season to taste. Drain off stock and serve carrots very hot.

MENU *13*

Leeks Fines Herbes

Serves 4   *40 calories per portion*

5ml | 1 level teaspoon mixed herbs, fresh or dried
5ml | 1 level teaspoon oregano, fresh or dried
Pinch tarragon, fresh or dried
Apple juice (optional)
450g | 1lb leeks
1.25ml | ¼ teaspoon oil

Soak dried herbs overnight in a little water or apple juice. Trim off and discard roots and green leaves from leeks. Dice leeks. Put a non-stick saucepan on to heat and brush with oil. Add leeks and stir-fry for 1 minute. Add the herbs and continue stir-frying until leeks are cooked (about 4–5 minutes). Serve hot.

MENUS 6 AND 10

Courgettes à la Provençale

Serves 4   *25 calories per portion*

350g | 12oz courgettes
125g | 4oz onions
1 clove garlic
227g | 8oz can tomatoes
5ml | 1 level teaspoon oregano, fresh or dried
Salt and pepper

Cut the courgettes into fingers, chop the onions and crush the garlic. Drain the tomato juice into a saucepan, add the onion and garlic, simmer for 5 minutes. Dice the tomatoes and add to the pan with oregano and courgettes. Season. Mix well. Cover pan and simmer for 15 minutes. Serve hot.

MENU 12

Risotto Rice

Serves 4   *115 calories per portion*

2 chicken stock cubes
275ml | ½ pint water
25g | 1oz onion
25g | 1oz mushrooms
125g | 4oz long-grain rice
Pinch saffron

Crumble stock cubes in water and bring to the boil. Dice the onion and mushrooms and put into a casserole dish with rice and saffron. Pour over the boiling stock, mix together and cover with lid or seal with foil. Bake in a preheated oven at 180°C/350°F, gas mark 4, for 30–40 minutes. Serve hot.

MENU 9

Salads

California Salad

Serves 1   *80 calories*

1 small orange
25g | 1oz cooked French beans
50g | 2oz slice fresh pineapple or 2 rings
pineapple canned in natural juice
1 stick celery
25g | 1oz onion
5ml | 1 teaspoon oil-free French dressing

Skin the orange and cut into thin slices.
Dice the beans, pineapple and celery.
Finely chop the onion. Mix all these
ingredients together with the French dressing. Refrigerate for 30 minutes to allow the
flavours to merge. Serve chilled.

MENU *2*

Mushroom and Cucumber Salad

Serves 1   *75 calories*

175g | 6oz cucumber
125g | 4oz button mushrooms
50g | 2oz shallots
5ml | 1 level teaspoon chopped chives
5ml | 1 teaspoon olive oil
30ml | 2 tablespoons white wine vinegar

Dice the cucumber and thinly slice the mushrooms. Finely chop the shallots and put into a mixing bowl with the other ingredients. Mix together and leave in the refrigerator overnight. Serve chilled.

MENU *3*

Orange and Celery Salad

Serves 1   *60 calories*

25g | 1oz cooked French beans
15g | ½oz onion
1 stick celery
25g | 1oz carrot
1 small orange
5ml | 1 teaspoon Waistline or Heinz
low-calorie salad dressing

Dice the beans, onion and celery. Grate the carrot and segment the orange. Mix all the ingredients except orange with the salad dressing. Put in a serving dish and garnish with the orange segments.

MENU *5*

Coleslaw Salad

Serves 1   *95 calories*

75g | 3oz Dutch or white cabbage
50g | 2oz carrot
50g | 2oz Spanish onion
15ml | 1 tablespoon Waistline or Heinz
low-calorie salad dressing
Salt and pepper

Finely shred the cabbage; grate carrot and chop onion. Mix with salad dressing. Season to taste and serve chilled.

MENUS *7* AND *9*

Chapter 6

HIGH STYLE/ LOW CALORIE RECIPES

Being on a diet does not mean that you have to be saintly all the time. If one of the joys in your life is to entertain friends to dinner, then attempts to cut this out completely could leave you feeling resentful and disinclined to continue your weight loss programme.

Your best plan is to choose one of the delicious menus that follow. Your friends will not even know (unless you boast the fact to them) that they are eating a low-calorie meal. And you can enjoy yourself in the knowledge that your diet is still intact, without feelings of guilt or remorse for indulging in dangerously high-calorie dishes.

Make your dinner party day a slightly naughty day – it is quite natural to have these occasionally – rather than trying to be very strict. If you eat 2,000 calories in one day you may not lose weight, but you will

67

not gain any either. You can always be strict on another day to make up. Keep the other meals on your dinner party day nicely low and you could afford even the highest calorie menu of those that follow – and have calories left over for a few drinks.

Each High Style/Low Calorie menu is followed by the recipes, unless they have already been used in Ragdale Dieting Menus (Chapter 2). In this case they are marked * if they are included in *Recipes for One* (remember to multiply quantities by four), ** if included in *Recipes for Freezing*, and some vegetables † are given in the *Vegetables and Salads* chapter.

The cost of preparing some of these High Style/Low Calorie meals at first glance may appear expensive, but if you add up the money *and* the calories that you save by cutting down on costly convenience foods, you will find the recipes good value both in nutritional terms and, of course, for the weight you will lose.

Menu 1

Serves 4   *700 calories per serving*

Asparagus and Cheese Dip

Poached Salmon and Hollandaise Sauce
Green Beans Fines Herbes †
Minted New Potatoes
Indienne Salad

Flamed Baked Banana

Asparagus and Cheese Dip

Serves 4   *60 calories per portion*

12 asparagus spears, fresh or frozen
25g / 1oz Danish blue cheese

68

2.5ml | ½ level teaspoon mustard powder
5ml | 1 level teaspoon chopped chives
15ml | 1 level tablespoon wine vinegar
150g | 5oz natural yogurt

Gently poach the asparagus spears in seasoned water until the base is tender. Allow to cool. Crush the blue cheese and mix with mustard and chives. Moisten with the vinegar and mix well into the yogurt. Chill and serve poured over the asparagus tips.

Poached Salmon

Serves 4   *270 calories per portion*

1½ litres | 2½ pints water
Bouquet garni
1 small onion
Salt and pepper
4 salmon cutlets (175g | 6oz each)

Bring the water to the boil, add the bouquet garni, whole onion and seasoning and simmer for 15 minutes. Add the salmon steaks and simmer very gently for a further 15 minutes. Test to see if salmon is cooked by pressing gently on the bone. If the bone comes out easily the salmon is cooked, if not simmer for a further 5 minutes and try again. Drain and serve with Hollandaise Sauce.

Hollandaise Sauce

Serves 4   *35 calories per portion*

125ml | 4fl oz white wine vinegar
Bay leaf
5ml | 1 level teaspoon crushed whole black peppercorns
2 egg yolks, size 3

Gently simmer the wine vinegar, bay leaf and pepper in a saucepan until the volume is reduced by half. Strain the liquid into a mixing bowl and add the egg yolks. Place the bowl over (but not touching) boiling water and whisk sauce vigorously until it is light and fluffy and slightly thickened. Continue whisking for a further 2–3 minutes. Pour into a jug and serve immediately.

Minted New Potatoes

Serves 4   *90 calories per portion*

450g | 1lb new potatoes
Salt
Fresh mint (or 5ml | 1 level teaspoon mint sauce)

Scrub potatoes and boil in salted water with mint until cooked. Serve in skins without adding butter or margarine. If you wish you can toss potatoes in a little soured cream – this will cost 30 calories for each 15ml / 1 level tablespoon. Serve hot.

Indienne Salad

Serves 4   *120 calories per portion*

125g | 4oz brown rice
Salt
50g | 2oz spring onions
50g | 2oz button mushrooms
½ red pepper
15ml | 1 level tablespoon Mild Madras curry powder
5ml | 1 level teaspoon chopped chives
30ml | 2 level tablespoons natural yogurt

Cook the brown rice in boiling salted water. Drain and cool in running cold water; drain again. Finely dice the onions, mushrooms and pepper and put into a bowl. Mix in the rice, curry powder, chives and yogurt. Serve cold.

Flamed Baked Banana

Serves 4   *90 calories per portion*

4 small bananas
30ml | 2 level tablespoons honey
150ml | 5fl oz water
25ml | 1fl oz rum

Bake bananas in skins at 180°C/350°F, gas mark 4, for 20 minutes. Slice along top side with knife and push gently on each side to push out flesh. Add honey to water in a small pan and bring to the boil. Add rum, then flame. While mixture is flaming pour it over bananas and serve immediately. *Note:* if you decide not to flame the rum, then add 10 calories to each serving.

═══ Menu 2 ═══

Serves 4   *715 calories per serving*

Apple and Pineapple Salad

Tournedos Anita
Leeks à la Provençale
Boiled carrots (450g / 1lb)
Duchesse Potatoes

Fresh Fruit Salad **

Apple and Pineapple Salad

Serves 4   *90 calories per portion*

1 small pineapple
2 eating apples
4 spring onions

5ml | 1 level teaspoon chopped chives, fresh
30ml | 2 level tablespoons chopped walnuts
30ml | 2 tablespoons low-calorie salad dressing
Lettuce

Cut off skin from the pineapple and cut flesh into small cubes. Wash, core and cube apples. Chop onions and put into a bowl with chives, walnuts, fruit and salad dressing. Mix together and serve on a bed of lettuce.

Tournedos Anita

Serves 4   *380 calories per portion*

4 fillet steaks (175g | 6oz each)
125g | 4oz chicken livers
125g | 4oz canned tomatoes
50g | 2oz diced shallots
50g | 2oz button mushrooms
50ml | 2fl oz brandy
5ml | 1 level teaspoon garlic salt
150ml | $\frac{1}{4}$ pint water
$\frac{1}{2}$ beef stock cube
15g | $\frac{1}{2}$oz crushed peppercorns

Trim off and discard all visible fat from steaks. Finely dice the chicken livers and put in a saucepan with the tomatoes, shallots and sliced button mushrooms. Add the brandy and garlic salt and bring to the boil; simmer for 5 minutes. Add the water and crumbled stock cube and simmer for 10 minutes more. Stud the fillet steaks with peppercorns and grill to taste. Cover with the sauce and serve.

Leeks à la Provençale

Serves 4   *40 calories per portion*

350g | 12oz leeks
125g | 4oz onions

1 clove garlic
227g | 8oz can tomatoes
5ml | 1 level teaspoon oregano, fresh or dried

Slice leeks, dice the onions and crush the garlic. Drain the tomato juice into a saucepan, add the onions and garlic, simmer for 5 minutes. Dice the tomatoes and add to the pan with oregano and leeks. Simmer for 15 minutes. Serve hot.

Duchesse Potatoes

Serves 4   *95 calories per portion*

350g | 12oz potatoes
1 egg yolk, size 3
5ml | 1 level teaspoon low-fat spread
Salt and pepper

Peel and boil potatoes. Cook until soft, then drain. Mash with egg yolk and low-fat spread, salt and pepper, then beat until smooth. Pipe potato mixture into a rosette on a non-stick baking tray. Bake at 190°C/ 375°F, gas mark 5, for about 10 minutes, until edges of potato start to brown. Serve hot.

Menu 3

Serves 4   *660 calories per serving*

Cucumber Vinaigrette

Tournedos au Poivre Vert
Pepperoni
Pommes de terre Marquises
Carottes Fines Herbes †

Melon with Stem Ginger *

Cucumber Vinaigrette

Serves 4   *20 calories per portion*

1 large cucumber
50ml | 2fl oz lemon juice
150ml | 5fl oz wine or cider vinegar
1 green pepper
3 sachets Sweet 'n' Low
275ml | 10fl oz unsweetened apple juice

Peel and slice the cucumber and soak in water and a teaspoon of the lemon juice for 1 hour. Drain the cucumber and put in a bowl with the vinegar. Mix in diced pepper, Sweet 'n' Low, apple juice and the rest of the lemon juice. Marinate for 1 hour and serve cucumbers drained and chilled. The marinade can be kept to serve as a salad dressing and costs 25 calories per quarter portion.

Tournedos au Poivre Vert

Serves 4   *380 calories per portion*

4 fillet steaks (175g | 6oz each)
1.25ml | ¼ teaspoon oil
125ml | 4fl oz dry white wine
30ml | 2 tablespoons brandy
30ml | 2 tablespoons green peppercorns
5ml | 1 level teaspoon chives, freeze-dried or fresh
50g | 2oz finely diced shallots
1 beef stock cube
5ml | 1 level teaspoon cornflour
275ml | ½ pint skimmed milk

Make sure all visible fat is trimmed off the steaks. Brush oil onto a non-stick pan and fry the steaks until cooked to your own personal taste. Remove from the pan and keep hot. Pour the wine and brandy into the pan and allow the alcohol to evaporate. Add the peppercorns, chives,

74

shallots and stock cube. Simmer for 2–3 minutes. Mix cornflour with milk, pour into pan and bring to the boil. Simmer for 5 minutes, stirring occasionally. Pour sauce over the steaks. Serve hot.

Pepperoni

Serves 4   *30 calories per portion*

125g | 4oz red peppers
125g | 4oz green peppers
125g | 4oz onions
50ml | 2fl oz dry white wine
5ml | 1 level teaspoon dried mixed herbs
1 clove garlic
227g | 8oz canned tomatoes

Thinly slice the peppers and onions; put into a non-stick saucepan with wine and herbs. Simmer for 2–3 minutes. Crush the garlic and add to pan with the tomato juice. Bring to the boil. Reduce the liquid by half by boiling and stirring vigorously. Dice the tomatoes and add to the sauce. Simmer for 5 minutes and serve hot.

Pommes de terre Marquises

Serves 4   *100 calories per portion*

350g | 12oz potatoes
1 egg yolk, size 3
5ml | 1 level teaspoon low-fat spread
1 tomato
5ml | 1 level teaspoon chives, fresh
Salt and pepper

Peel and boil potatoes. Cook until soft, then drain. Mash with egg yolk and low-fat spread, salt and pepper, and beat until very smooth. Pipe potato mixture in rosettes on to a non-stick baking tray. Make a hole in the top of each rosette with a teaspoon. Skin and finely dice the tomato and mix with chopped chives. Divide the mixture between potatoes putting mixture into the hole at top. Bake at 190°C/375°F, gas mark 5, for about 10 minutes until edges of potato start to brown. Serve hot.

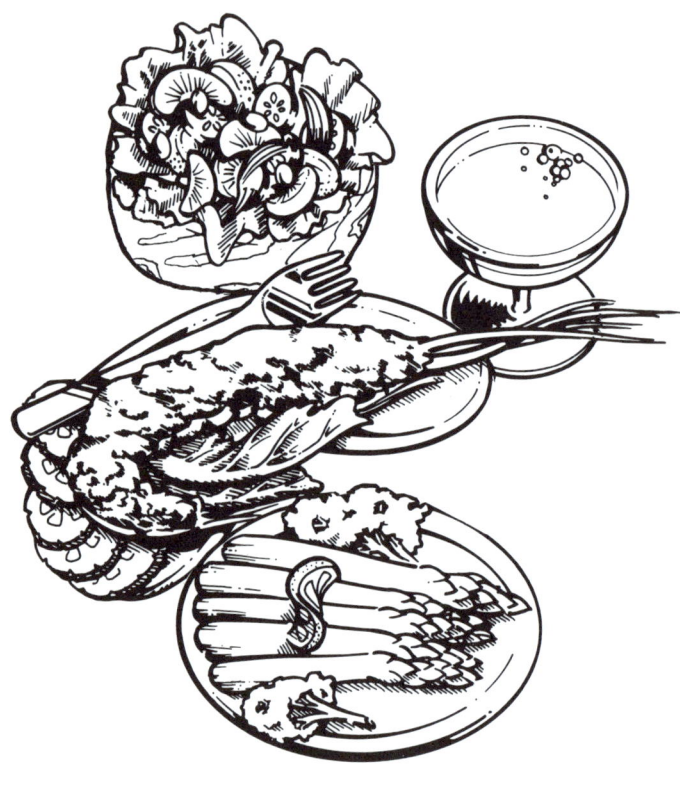

Menu 4

Serves 4   *550 calories per serving*

Cucumber Soup

Lobster Thermidor
Super Salad
Boiled asparagus (225g / 8oz)

Peach Melba *

Cucumber Soup

Serves 4   *70 calories per portion*

2 large cucumbers
50g / 2oz onion
15g / ½oz low-fat spread
7g / ¼oz plain flour
275ml / ½ pint water
1 chicken stock cube
125g / 4oz natural yogurt
5ml / 1 level teaspoon chopped parsley
Salt and pepper

Peel and dice the cucumbers and onion. Melt the low-fat spread in a pan and stir in the flour. Gradually add the onion and cucumber. Stir in the water and chicken stock cube, mixing well. Bring to the boil and simmer for 45 minutes. Cool slightly then purée in a blender. Chill and mix in the yogurt and parsley. Season to taste. Serve chilled.

Lobster Thermidor

Serves 4   *230 calories per portion*

2 lobsters (350g / 12oz each)
225g / 8oz prawns, fresh or frozen
50g / 2oz shallots
50ml / 2fl oz dry white wine
15ml / 1 tablespoon brandy
5ml / 1 level teaspoon dry English mustard
275ml / ½ pint skimmed milk
15ml / 1 level tablespoon arrowroot
Salt and pepper
50g / 2oz Edam cheese, grated
5ml / 1 level teaspoon chopped parsley

Cut the lobsters in half down the backbone; remove and discard stomach and intestines. Remove flesh and dice. Wash the shells thoroughly. Crack open the claws. Put all flesh into a saucepan and add prawns, chopped shallots and white wine. Simmer gently for 5 minutes, then add brandy. Mix in mustard and all but two tablespoons skimmed milk. Bring to the boil and simmer for 5 minutes. Mix arrowroot with remaining milk and add to pan with seasoning. Stir until thickened. Spoon mixture into the shells and sprinkle with cheese. Grill until the cheese browns. Sprinkle with parsley and serve immediately.

Super Salad

Serves 4   *70 calories per portion*

125g | 4oz courgettes
125g | 4oz strawberries
50g | 2oz onion
1 orange
25g | 1oz salted peanuts
5ml | 1 level teaspoon dried mixed herbs
1 lemon

Thinly slice the courgettes and strawberries. Slice the onion; peel and segment the orange. Mix together in a bowl with peanuts. Sprinkle with herbs and squeeze over the lemon juice. Serve slightly chilled.

Menu 5

Serves 4   *585 calories per serving*

Mushrooms with Garlic

Chicken Cacciatore
Bean Sprouts à la Provençale
Stuffed Aubergines
Sauté Potatoes

Brandied Oranges

Mushrooms with Garlic

Serves 4   *20 calories per portion*

575g | 1lb 4oz large cap mushrooms
Sprinkle of garlic salt
1 lemon
2.5ml | ½ teaspoon oil
Lettuce

Remove stems from mushrooms and put caps on a grill tray. Sprinkle with garlic salt. Squeeze over lemon juice and brush with oil. Grill for 5 minutes under a hot grill. Serve hot on a bed of sliced lettuce.

Chicken Cacciatore

Serves 4   *200 calories per portion*

4 chicken breasts (175g | 6oz each)
125g | 4oz canned tomatoes
125g | 4oz button onions
125g | 4oz button mushrooms
125ml | 4fl oz red wine
5ml | 1 level teaspoon dried oregano
5ml | 1 level teaspoon dried marjoram
Pinch dried sage
2 chicken stock cubes
575ml | 1 pint water
15ml | 1 level tablespoon cornflour
Salt and pepper

Remove skin from chicken breasts and place in a casserole dish. Dice the tomatoes and put in saucepan with their juice, onions, mushrooms and red wine. Bring to the boil and simmer for 5 minutes. Add the herbs, stock cubes and water. Then bring back to the boil. Mix cornflour with a little cold water and add to sauce to thicken. Season to taste. Pour sauce over chicken and cook at 180°C/350°F, gas mark 4, for 45 minutes. Serve hot.

Bean Sprouts à la Provençale

Serves 4   *30 calories per portion*

350g | 12oz bean sprouts
125g | 4oz onions
1 clove garlic
227g | 8oz can tomatoes
5ml | 1 level teaspoon oregano, fresh or dried

Wash and drain bean sprouts, dice the onions and crush the garlic. Drain the tomato juice into a saucepan, add the onions and garlic, simmer for 5 minutes. Dice the tomatoes and add to the pan with oregano and bean sprouts. Simmer for 15 minutes. Serve hot.

Stuffed Aubergines

Serves 4   *120 calories per portion*

2 medium aubergines
125g | 4oz onions
125g | 4oz button mushrooms
1 medium green pepper
1.25ml | ¼ teaspoon oil
5ml | 1 level teaspoon chopped sage
125g | 4oz Edam cheese, grated

Cut the aubergines in half, scoop out the seeds and bake at 190°C/375°F, gas mark 5, for 10 minutes. Finely dice the onions, mushrooms and pepper. Brush a non-stick pan with oil and cook onions, mushrooms, pepper and sage until soft but not browned. Remove aubergines from the oven, stuff with vegetable mixture, top with cheese and bake for a further 10 minutes until the cheese goes golden brown. Serve hot.

Sauté Potatoes

Serves 4   *90 calories per portion*

350g | 12oz potatoes
125g | 4oz onions
1.25ml | ¼ teaspoon oil

Boil potatoes in skins. Cool under running water and peel as thinly as possible. Slice thickly. Peel and thinly slice onions. Brush a non-stick pan with oil and add potatoes and onions. Cook over a high heat, tossing vegetables gently, until they brown. Serve hot.

Brandied Oranges

Serves 4   *70 calories per portion*

4 medium oranges
Sweet 'n' Low, optional
20ml | 4 teaspoons brandy

Peel and slice oranges. Sprinkle with Sweet 'n' Low and brandy. Leave in fridge for 30 minutes to an hour and serve chilled.

Menu 6

Serves 4   *775 calories per serving*

Carrot Kugelhof

Tournedos Chasseur
Boiled cauliflower (225g / 8oz)
Boiled green beans (225g / 8oz)
Sauté Potatoes (see Menu 5)

Fresh Strawberries or Raspberries
with Yogurt

Carrot Kugelhof

Serves 4   *255 calories per portion*

1 clove garlic
125g / 4oz onions
125g / 4oz mushrooms
30ml / 2 level tablespoons low-fat spread
225g / 8oz carrots
425ml / ¾ pint water
3 chicken stock cubes
6 eggs (size 3)
2.5ml / ½ level teaspoon turmeric
Salt and pepper
75g / 3oz Edam cheese, grated
30ml / 2 level tablespoons chopped parsley

Crush the garlic; dice onions and mush-rooms. Cook in a saucepan with low-fat spread. Add diced carrots and boiling water with stock cubes. Cover and simmer for 20 minutes. Remove cover and boil vigorously, stirring continuously, until the water evaporates. Put vegetables in a liquidizer with 2 eggs and make into a purée. Add turmeric, salt, pepper and remaining eggs. Blend thoroughly. Add cheese and parsley, then put mixture in a casserole dish. Stand the dish in a pan of water to come half-way up the sides of the dish. Bake at 180°C/350°F, gas mark 4, for 1 hour. Serve hot.

Tournedos Chasseur

Serves 4   *360 calories per portion*

4 fillet steaks (175g | 6oz each)
125g | 4oz onions
2 medium tomatoes
225g | 8oz button mushrooms
125ml | 4fl oz dry white wine
Pinch garlic salt
10ml | 2 level teaspoons tomato purée
275ml | ½ pint water
1 chicken stock cube
5ml | 1 level teaspoon cornflour

Trim all visible fat from steaks. Dice the onions and tomatoes and slice the mushrooms. Put the wine into a saucepan and bring to the boil. Add the vegetables and simmer for 2 minutes. Stir in garlic salt, tomato purée, water and stock cube. Simmer for 10 minutes. Mix cornflour with a little cold water and add to sauce to thicken. Grill the steaks and serve topped with sauce.

Strawberries or Raspberries with Yogurt

Serves 4   *50 calories per portion*

450g | 1lb strawberries or raspberries, fresh
Lemon juice
150g | 5oz natural yogurt

Wash and hull fruit and arrange in serving dishes. Sprinkle with a little lemon juice and top with yogurt.

Menu 7

Serves 4   *394 calories per serving*

Grapefruit Xérès *

Lobster à la Provençale
Courgettes Fines Herbes
Boiled runner beans (225g / 8oz)

Peach in Brandy

Courgettes Fines Herbes

Serves 4   *15 calories per portion*

*5ml / 1 level teaspoon chopped chives,
fresh or dried
5ml / 1 level teaspoon chopped basil,
fresh or dried
5ml / 1 level teaspoon chopped oregano,
fresh or dried
Apple juice (optional)
350g / 12oz courgettes
1.25ml / ¼ teaspoon oil
Salt and pepper*

Soak dried herbs overnight in water or apple juice. Wash and slice courgettes. Brush a non-stick pan with oil. Allow to get hot, then add courgettes. Gently toss for 2–3 minutes without colouring. Sprinkle with herbs and seasoning and cook so that courgettes are al dente (firm to eat).

Lobster à la Provençale

Serves 4   *265 calories per portion*

125g | 4oz brown rice
2 cooked lobsters (350g | 12oz each)
225g | 8oz scampi
50g | 2oz shallots
125ml | 4fl oz dry white wine
4 firm tomatoes
2.5ml | ½ level teaspoon garlic salt
125ml | 4fl oz tomato juice

Boil the brown rice. Remove and discard the stomachs and intestines from lobsters. Remove meat and cut into roughly the same size as the scampi. Wash shells and put on serving dish. Put fish into a saucepan with diced shallots and wine and simmer for 4–5 minutes. Skin and dice the tomatoes and add to the pan with garlic salt and tomato juice. Continue to simmer for a further 15 minutes. Spoon provençal mixture back into shells and serve with rice.

Peach in Brandy

Serves 4   *65 calories per portion*

4 ripe peaches
250ml | 9fl oz water
4 packets Sweet 'n' Low
30ml | 2 tablespoons brandy
5ml | 1 level teaspoon arrowroot

Stone the peaches and cut into thin slices. Put the water into a saucepan and bring to the boil. Add the Sweet 'n' Low. Put sliced peaches into a non-stick frying pan, add brandy and heat gently. Add the sweetened boiling water. Blend arrowroot with a little cold water and add to peaches. Simmer for 4–5 minutes and serve hot.

Menu 8

Serves 4   *640 calories per serving*

Baked Vegetable Pie

Grilled Salmon Steaks Doria
Aubergines à la Provençale
Boiled broccoli (225g / 8oz)
Minted New Potatoes (see Menu 1)

Blackcurrant Brulée

Baked Vegetable Pie

Serves 4   *30 calories per portion*

125g / 4oz onions
125g / 4oz courgettes
125g / 4oz aubergine
2 firm tomatoes
227g / 8oz can tomatoes
275ml / $\frac{1}{2}$ pint water
1 chicken stock cube

Thinly slice all the vegetables and tomatoes, drain the juice from the canned tomatoes. Layer a casserole dish with first the onions, then canned tomatoes, courgettes, aubergine and top with fresh tomatoes. Mix the tomato juice with water and stock cube and pour over vegetables. Bake at 200°C/400°F, gas mark 6, for 40 minutes. Serve hot.

Grilled Salmon Steaks Doria

Serves 4   *335 calories per portion*

4 salmon steaks (175g / 6oz each)
1.25ml / $\frac{1}{4}$ teaspoon oil
50g / 2oz onion
125ml / 4oz cucumber
5ml / 1 level teaspoon chopped chives
125ml / 4fl oz dry white wine

15g / ½oz cornflour
275ml / ½ pint skimmed milk

Brush the salmon steaks lightly with oil and grill for about 10 minutes each side. The steak is cooked when the bone easily comes out when pressed. Finely dice the onion and cucumber. Put into a saucepan with chives and wine and simmer for 2–3 minutes. Mix the cornflour with the milk and add to sauce to thicken. Simmer for 10 minutes and serve over salmon steaks.

Aubergines à la Provençale

Serves 4   *25 calories per portion*

350g / 12oz aubergine
125g / 4oz onions
1 clove garlic
227g / 8oz can tomatoes
5ml / 1 level teaspoon dried oregano

Slice aubergine, dice the onions and crush the garlic. Drain the tomato juice into a saucepan, add the onions and garlic, simmer for 5 minutes. Dice the tomatoes and add to the pan with oregano and aubergine. Simmer for 15 minutes. Serve hot.

Blackcurrant Brulée

Serves 4   *95 calories per portion*

275g / 10oz blackcurrants, fresh or frozen
120ml / 8 tablespoons water
10ml / 2 level teaspoons cornflour
32 drops Sweetex liquid
142g / 5oz carton blackcurrant yogurt
20ml / 4 level teaspoons soft light brown sugar
15g / ½oz flaked almonds

Place blackcurrants and water in a saucepan. Cover and cook gently until soft. Blend cornflour with a little extra water to make a smooth paste. Add to the blackcurrants and bring to the boil, stirring continuously. Cook for 1–2 minutes. Add the Sweetex and leave until cold. Divide between four small heatproof dishes. Spread yogurt over blackcurrants and chill. Sprinkle sugar and almonds on top and grill for a few minutes until the sugar melts and almonds turn brown. Serve immediately.

Menu 9

Serves 4   *545 calories per serving*

Stuffed Tomatoes

Casserole of Quail
Duchesse Potatoes (see Menu 2)
Marrow à la Provençale
Leeks Fines Herbes †

Pineapple and Kirsch *

Stuffed Tomatoes

Serves 4   *60 calories per portion*

4 firm tomatoes
125g / 4oz cottage cheese
5ml / 1 level teaspoon chopped chives, fresh
5ml / 1 level teaspoon chopped parsley, fresh
Finely grated zest of ½ lemon
1 orange
Salt and pepper
Lettuce, cucumber, watercress

Cut tops off tomatoes, remove seeds. Crush the lumps out of the cottage cheese with a fork, add the chives, parsley and lemon zest. Mix well together. Peel and chop the orange. Gently fold into the stuffing mixture and add seasoning. Rest in the fridge for 15 minutes for the flavours to blend. Use to stuff tomatoes. Serve with a green salad of lettuce, cucumber and watercress.

Casserole of Quail

Serves 4   *275 calories per portion*

8 small quail
1 small onion, 1 stick celery
125g / 4oz button mushrooms
125ml / 4fl oz dry white wine
125g / 4oz seedless white grapes
550ml / 1 pint water
2 chicken stock cubes
15ml / 1 level tablespoon cornflour

Skin the quail and put in a casserole dish. Finely dice the onion, celery and button mushrooms, put into a saucepan, pour over the wine and simmer for 5 minutes. Add the grapes, water and crumbled stock cubes. Bring to the boil and reduce by half. Pour over the quail, seal dish tightly with foil and bake in a preheated oven at 180°C/350°F, gas mark 4, for 20 minutes. Pour the juices into a saucepan and bring to the boil. Mix cornflour with a little cold water and add to juices to thicken. Simmer for 5 minutes and pour over the quail. Serve hot.

Marrow à la Provençale

Serves 4   *30 calories per portion*

350g / 2oz marrow
125g / 4oz onions, 1 clove garlic
227g / 8oz can tomatoes
5ml / 1 level teaspoon oregano, fresh or dried

Slice marrow, dice the onions and crush the garlic. Drain the tomato juice into a saucepan, add the onions and garlic, simmer for 5 minutes. Dice the tomatoes and add to the pan with oregano and marrow. Simmer for 15 minutes. Serve hot.

Chapter 7

DRINKS

You can drink as much liquid as you wish when you are dieting, as long as you include any of the calories in your daily total. Water, whether from the tap or out of a bottle, contains no calories and can be drunk freely. The body very efficiently gets rid of any excess water.

Alcohol will contribute nothing but calories to your diet and, of course, can be damaging to your health, so we recommend that you drink it in moderation. Here we show you what interesting cocktails you can make by combining low-calorie squashes, fruit juice and mixes – yet with no alcohol.

American Bitters

Serves 1   *1 calorie*

Coat glass with Angostura bitters. Add a bottle of low-calorie ginger ale and garnish with ice and lemon.

Gatsby Liner

Serves 1   *3 calories*

Add 25ml / 1fl oz Chekwate Lime to a bottle of low-calorie ginger ale. Garnish with ice and lemon.

Sh Sh Super

Serves 1   *12 calories*

Coat glass with Angostura bitters. Add a bottle of low-calorie tonic water. Garnish with ice and lemon.

Contrary Mary

Serves 1   *36 calories*

To one bottle of tomato juice add 25ml / 1fl oz PLJ and a dash of Worcestershire sauce. Garnish with ice and lemon and top up with low-calorie tonic water.

Golden Sunrise

Serves 1   *6 calories*

To 25ml / 1fl oz Chekwate Orange add one can of One Cal Lemon and Lime. Garnish with ice and orange.

Orange Fizz

Serves 1   *52 calories*

To 125ml / 4fl oz fresh orange juice add low-calorie lemonade. Garnish with ice and lemon.

Ragdale Special

Serves 1   *3 calories*

To 25ml / 1fl oz Chekwate Lime add a bottle of Diet Pepsi. Garnish with ice and lemon.

Silver Cloud

Serves 1   *5 calories*

To 25ml / 1fl oz Chekwate Grapefruit add a can of One Cal Lemon and Lime. Garnish with ice and lemon.

Grapefruit and Lime Surprise

Serves 1   *11 calories*

To 25ml / 1fl oz Chekwate Grapefruit and 25ml / 1fl oz Chekwate Lime add a bottle of low-calorie lemonade. Garnish with ice and lemon.

Robin's Special

Serves 1   *2 calories*

Coat glass with Angostura bitters. Top up with One Cal Orange and garnish with ice and orange slice.

Orange Dash

Serves 1   *16 calories*

To 25ml / 1fl oz Chekwate Orange add a bottle of Slimline Lemonade. Garnish with ice and orange slice.

Fruit Cooler

Serves 4   *75 calories per portion*

575ml / 1 pint skimmed milk
150g / 5½oz carton natural yogurt
50ml / 2fl oz measure Chekwate Fruit Cordial (any flavour)
Sweet 'n' Low, optional

Mix together milk and yogurt and pour over the cordial. Sweeten with Sweet 'n' Low if needed.

Chapter 8

HISTORICAL PROFILE OF RAGDALE HALL

Mellow red brick, centuries old green sward, banks of old English roses, ancient trees: these are the heritage of Ragdale Hall.

The Doomsday Book records Rakedale or Rakendale as a manor or measure of land consisting of six ploughshares employing six ploughs at a value of 16 pence. More glorious days began when William the Conqueror bestowed this fertile and beautiful land in the heart of Leicestershire on one of his supporters, Hugh Lupus, Earl of Chester.

In later generations, the wealthy aristocrats who resided at the Manor of Ragdale remained staunch supporters of the reigning monarch. Sir Robert Shirley supported

King John against the Barons and the Great Charter, and stood a mourner when John's heart was buried in the nearby village of Croxton Kerrial.

In the Wars of the Roses, a later Sir Robert gladly welcomed the dangerous distinction of going into battle disguised as the king so as to decoy the enemy. Over his armour, he wore a surcoat embroidered with the Royal Henry IV armorial bearings – a brave stratagem that cost him his life.

Another descendant, also a Sir Robert, supported King Charles I in the civil war against Cromwell, languishing in the Tower for many years before he died. King Charles II rewarded Sir Robert's son by raising him to the peerage, creating him first Baron Ferrers. The family's peaceful enjoyment of their heritage echoed the more peaceful and serene stability of the Crown thereafter.

Ragdale Hall became a hunting lodge for the royal families and aristocrats attracted to the Quorn and Belvoir Hunts close by; and when the ancient manor house burned down in the 18th century, the then Viscount Tamworth and Earl Ferrers lost no time in building a handsome new establishment whose castellated top storey and mellow red brick reflected the fashionable architecture of the day.

This is the building – mature, spacious, not quite 200 years old – that welcomes visitors to Ragdale today.

Index